METANOIA

A PROFOUND TRANSFORMATION

VIKRAM VARAKHEDI

"

This book is dedicated to my beloved family, Gururaj Varakhedi, Vidya Varakhedi, and Anjana. Your unwavering love and support have been the driving force behind my every endeavor. From the very beginning, your encouragement and belief in me have been the solid foundation upon which I have built my life and my work. I am forever grateful for the countless sacrifices you have made to help me pursue my dreams. This book serves as a small token of my appreciation for everything you have done.

To my father, Gururaj Varakhedi, your wisdom and guidance have shaped me into the person I am today. You have been my constant source of inspiration, always pushing me to reach for the stars and reminding me of the importance of perseverance. Thank you for being there for me every step of the way.

To my mother, Vidya Varakhedi, your love and nurturing nature have nurtured my creativity and ambition. You have instilled in me the values of compassion and determination, and I am grateful for the strength you have given me. Your unwavering support has been my pillar of strength throughout my journey.

And to my wife, Anjana, you are my rock and my biggest cheerleader. Your love, patience, and belief in me have been instrumental in my successes. Your unwavering support and understanding have made all the difference, and I am grateful for the love and stability you bring to our family.

Together, you have been my constant source of inspiration and a reminder of what truly matters in life—love, family, and the pursuit of dreams. Thank you for being there for me, for shaping me into the person I am today, and for being the cornerstone of my happiness. This book is dedicated to each of you, as a testament to the profound impact you have had on my life."

ᚦᚦᚦ

Contents

Contents

Preface

Dear Reader,

Welcome to "Metanoia," a book dedicated to the transformative power that lies within each of us. It is my sincere belief that true success in life begins with an inner transformation—a shift in mindset, habits, and perspectives—that ultimately propels us towards achieving our goals and aspirations.

In the pages of this book, I invite you to join me on a journey of self-discovery and personal growth. Drawing from my own experiences of feeling stuck and unfulfilled, I share the practical advice and guidance that helped me break free from the chains of stagnation and embark on a path towards success.

"Metanoia" is not a magic recipe for overnight riches or instant fame. Instead, it offers a collection of 15 transformative habits that, when embraced and practiced consistently, have the power to create lasting change in your life. These habits are not meant to be rigidly followed in a specific order, but rather to be tailored to your unique circumstances and incorporated into your daily routine at your own pace.

Through the anecdotes, lessons, and guidelines shared within these pages, I aim to inspire you to take control of your destiny and unleash your full potential. Whether you seek recognition in your professional endeavors, financial abundance, or simply a deeper sense of fulfillment and purpose, "Metanoia" serves as a roadmap for your personal evolution.

I firmly believe that anyone can make meaningful changes in their life that lead to greater recognition, increased earnings, and a profound sense of satisfaction. By cultivating a growth mindset, adopting empowering habits, and embracing the power of self-reflection, you can embark on a transformative journey that will unlock the doors to success.

As you immerse yourself in the wisdom and insights shared in this book, I encourage you to approach each chapter with an open mind and a willingness to challenge your current beliefs and limitations. Together, let us embark on this transformative quest, knowing that within each of us lies the capacity for greatness.

May "Metanoia" be the catalyst that ignites the fire of change within you and propels you towards a future filled with accomplishment, fulfillment, and joy.

With gratitude,

Vikram Varakhedi

ᕤᕤᕤ

Acknowledgements

As I reflect on the journey that led me to this moment, I am filled with gratitude for the many incredible individuals who have played a significant role in my life and supported me along the way. I would like to express my deepest appreciation to those who have made a lasting impact on my personal and professional growth.

To my friends, thank you for your unwavering support, encouragement, and for being there for me through thick and thin. Your friendship has been a constant source of inspiration and joy, and I am grateful for the memories we have created together.

I extend my heartfelt thanks to the mentors, teachers, and colleagues who have shared their wisdom, guidance, and expertise with me. Your valuable insights and belief in my abilities have propelled me forward, helping me overcome challenges and reach new heights. Your contributions have shaped my journey in ways I could never have imagined.

I would also like to express my gratitude to the readers of this book. Your willingness to explore new ideas and perspectives is greatly appreciated. It is my sincere hope that the knowledge and strategies shared within these pages will empower you to achieve your own success and personal growth.

To all those who have touched my life in various ways, whether through a kind word, a helping hand, or a moment of inspiration, I am deeply grateful. Each interaction, no matter how small, has had a profound impact on my journey, and I am humbled by your presence.

Finally, I want to acknowledge the guiding force that has been with me throughout this journey. Whether you believe in the universe, a higher power, or the interconnectedness of all things, I am grateful for the opportunities and blessings that have come my way.

This book stands as a testament to the collective support and contributions of all those who have influenced my path. I am honored and indebted to each and every one of you for your presence in my life.

ƿƿƿ

Prologue

The Spark to Transform

"The mind is everything. What you think you become." – Lord Krishna

ᐯᐯᐯ

I had been working at the same 9 to 5 desk job for over three years now, and while I loved my work, I couldn't shake off the feeling that I could be doing so much more. I was always praised by my bosses for my abilities and approach, and I took pride in being a good employee who could complete tasks in the stipulated time. My salary was decent, and the perks were nice, but I couldn't help feeling like I was stuck in a rut.

Every day felt like a repeat of the previous one. I would wake up early, shave, clean myself up, grab a quick breakfast, and rush to work. I'd spend my entire day at the desk until lunchtime, take a few coffee breaks, and then continue working until 5:30 PM. I'd take the same bus route or drive the same roads back home, and catch up with news, sports or watch a TV series. It felt like I was living the same day over and over again.

The thought of being trapped in this monotonous routine started to eat away at me, slowly but surely. As time went on, it became harder and harder to ignore. One morning my boss delivered the news about my solo trip to Mumbai to address the difficult client, my heart dropped into my stomach. The weight of the responsibility felt suffocating, and I couldn't help but feel a sense of dread wash over me. But as the initial shock subsided, I began to see it as an opportunity to prove myself. Maybe, just maybe, this was the chance I needed to show my worth and make a name for myself in the company and also, I started to see this as an opportunity to break away from the stereotype.

I was excited about the opportunity to break free from the stereotype routine at least for a week. I flew to Mumbai with high hopes, hoping that this trip would change everything. As soon as I arrived, I felt a sense of adventure and excitement that I hadn't felt in years. The bustling city, the new sights, and the unfamiliar culture were all so exhilarating.

For the first time in a long time, I felt alive. I was no longer just going through the motions, but rather experiencing something entirely new. The trip helped me realize that there was so much more to life than just the same old routine. And while it wasn't easy to leave behind the comfort and familiarity of my job, I knew it was time to take a chance and try something new.

I must admit, dear reader, that my visit to Mumbai was nothing short of a godsend. It was as if a fresh, gushing water had come to quench the thirst of my barren dreams, and I felt rejuvenated in an instant.

As I arrived in Mumbai, I was assigned a desk at the client's office and was stationed there for the next 8-10 days. And let me tell you, dear reader, it was exactly what I needed. Suddenly, I felt more energetic, more alive.

As someone who values hard work, I recognize the importance of finding a balance between work and rest. Taking breaks and recharging is essential to avoid burnout, especially when striving to achieve our goals. With the weekend approaching, I looked forward to exploring Mumbai on Saturday and taking some time to relax in my hotel room on Sunday

And that's precisely what I did. I woke up on Sunday morning, sipped on my tea, and headed down to the lobby for breakfast. Mumbai's special Misal Pav and some Poha - it was nothing short of a gastronomic delight.

When I returned to my hotel room, I was greeted by the sight of a freshly cleaned room with a bed set up so precisely that it seemed a shame to even touch it. So, I sat down on the chair adjacent to the bed, admiring a beautiful painting hung on the wall.

As I sat there lost in my thoughts, I couldn't help but notice the impeccable job that the housekeeping staff had done. So, I stepped out of my room to see if I could find the person responsible for cleaning it.

And there he was, a middle-aged man with greying hair, cleaning the adjacent room. I smiled at him and asked if he had cleaned my room. He seemed to panic for a moment before admitting that he had indeed cleaned my room.

I reassured him that there was no problem and went on to compliment him on the precision of his work. He smiled and told me that he had been doing this job for the past ten years. And that's when it hit me.

As I chatted with him, I couldn't help but feel a sense of kinship. His words, his story - they resonated with me on a deep level. Despite our different professions, I felt as though I was in his shoes.

I left him a small tip and closed the door to my room, lost in my thoughts, I comforted myself into the chair and picked up the pencil and started scribbling away on a notepad. This short conversation had left me pondering, and I knew that I had to put my thoughts down on paper.

As I sat there, scribbling away, I couldn't help but wonder what the future held for both of us. Would he continue doing the same job day in and day out, just like I had been doing for the past three years? Or would he find the courage to pursue something else?

It was a lazy Sunday, but it had given me a lot to think about. And as I sat there, I couldn't help but feel a sense of gratitude - for this chance encounter, for the gushing fresh water that had rejuvenated my soul, and for the newfound energy that would carry me through the rest of my time in Mumbai. Staring at the painting on the wall and pondering the words of the cleaner who had made up my bed, I knew that I could not let myself get stuck in a rut. I wanted to flow like a stream, to constantly be moving and growing, rather than stagnating in one place.

With the title "I do not want to get stuck" in mind, I started brainstorming ways to prevent my life from becoming stagnant. As I jotted down my ideas, I noticed that my list was quickly growing, with each point feeling equally important. After some consideration, I decided to condense my ideas and merge some of them to create a more manageable list of 15 rules to follow in order to change the course of my life.

Over the course of the next 9 months, I applied each of those points to my life in every possible situation. I worked tirelessly to transform myself, to become the best version of myself that I could be.

As I delved deeper into each of the 15 rules that I had set for myself, I felt a profound shift in my life. To solidify my understanding and garner more insights, I shared my thoughts with my close friends, mentors, professors, and teachers. In an effort to pay it forward, I also offered my perspective to my peers and colleagues, and they were able to apply my suggestions to their own lives.

In this process, I was humbled to receive feedback and suggestions from my acquaintances and mentors, which further enriched my learning. As a result, my job profile transformed, and I began to cultivate healthier and more fulfilling relationships. I felt a renewed sense of purpose and direction in my life, and my overall sense of self underwent a positive transformation. I realized that collective efforts, coupled with a willingness to learn and grow, can lead to incredible results.

And as I looked back on that lazy Sunday morning in my hotel room in Mumbai, I knew that it had been a turning point for me. The moment when I had decided to take control of my life and chart a new course, to flow like a stream rather than becoming stagnant and stuck.

For I had learned that the key to success was not just hard work, but the willingness to constantly evolve and grow, to never be satisfied with the status quo. And as I continued to move forward, I knew that I would always remember that fateful day in Mumbai as the moment when I had truly begun to live.

I am thrilled to embark on this transformative journey with you, as we delve into the 15 points that I have meticulously organized into chapters within the pages of "Metanoia." These points serve as a guide for achieving personal growth and avoiding the stagnation that can hinder our progress.

To provide you with a comprehensive understanding, I have invested significant time and effort in conducting extensive research and engaging in thought-provoking discussions with diverse individuals. These conversations have ranged from healthy debates to finding common ground or respectfully disagreeing. Along the way, I have encountered individuals who have successfully applied these points, while others may have encountered obstacles and halted their progress.

What I have learned through this process is that personal growth and change are highly subjective. What works wonders for one person may not resonate with another. As such, I invite you to approach each chapter of this book with an open mind and heart, fully aware that these points are not a universal solution. Instead, they serve as invaluable tools that can guide you on your personal journey towards profound transformation and self-fulfillment.

In the following chapters, we will explore these 15 points in detail, uncovering the potential they hold to positively impact your life. Each point is designed to inspire self-reflection, encourage positive change, and foster personal development. It is my hope that you will find resonance and applicability in these points, adapting them to suit your unique circumstances and aspirations.

"Metanoia" is more than just a book; it is an invitation to embark on a transformative adventure. Together, we will navigate the complexities of personal growth, embracing the profound changes that await us. Through introspection, thoughtful consideration, and the application of these points, we will uncover new perspectives and possibilities, ultimately leading us towards a life of fulfillment and purpose.

So, let us embark on this remarkable journey of self-discovery and empowerment, as we explore the 15 points that hold the potential to unlock your truest potential. Open your heart and mind, for the adventure awaits within the pages of "Metanoia."

ᗡᗡᗡ

PROLOGUE

ONE

Mastering the Clock: Effective Strategies for Time Management

———❦———

"Your time is limited, don't waste it living someone else's life." - Steve Jobs.

❧❧❧

As I sat down to write this chapter, I couldn't help but think of how valuable time is. We all have the same amount of time in a day, yet some people seem to accomplish so much more than others. So, how do they do it? It's simple: they manage their time effectively.

As a young teenager, I found myself struggling to manage my time effectively. Despite my desire to learn a new musical instrument, I often found myself distracted by television or hanging out with friends for hours on end, leaving little time for anything else.

One day, my music teacher asked me if I had practiced the tune he had taught me a few classes earlier. Embarrassed, I admitted that I hadn't found the time to do so. It was then that my teacher pulled out a sheet of music notes and drew an empty jar, launching into a powerful metaphor that I would remember for years to come.

He explained by drawing an empty jar that it represented my time and how I chose to use it. He then drew large rocks, explaining that they represented important tasks with the highest priority. Next, he drew pebbles, which he mentioned were secondary tasks that needed to be done but weren't as important. After that, he drew sand, representing all the little things that can easily fill up our time if we're not careful. Finally, he explained that the water symbolized everything else in our lives.

At the time, I didn't fully grasp the significance of what my teacher was trying to teach me. But as I grew older, I began to understand the importance of prioritizing my time and focusing on the most important tasks first. Just like the jar, my time is finite and I need to make the most of it by focusing on what truly matters.

The lesson my music teacher taught me all those years ago has stayed with me ever since. It's a simple but powerful reminder that we all have a limited amount of time in our lives, and it's up to us to use it wisely. By focusing on the big rocks and prioritizing our time, we can achieve great things and make the most of every moment.

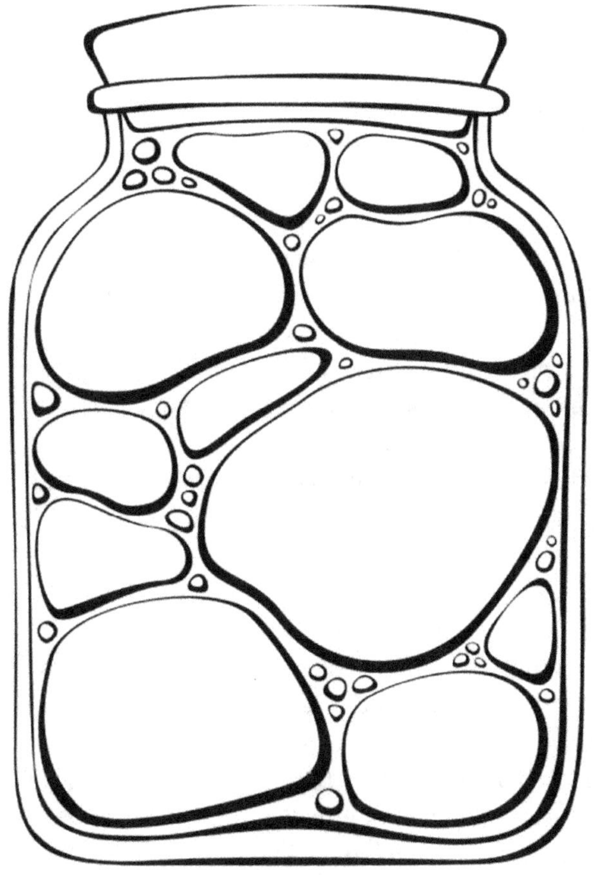

Effective time management vent is a crucial skill for achieving success in both personal and professional life. Over the years, many world-famous universities have conducted research and case studies on this topic, providing valuable insights and best practices for managing time effectively.

One of the most well-known studies was conducted by Harvard Business School, which found that effective time management leads to better decision-making, increased productivity, and reduced stress levels. The study also showed that prioritizing tasks and delegating responsibilities are essential for managing time efficiently.

Another study by the University of California, Irvine, found that it takes an average of 23 minutes and 15 seconds to refocus on a task after being interrupted. This study underscores the importance of limiting distractions and interruptions to improve time management.

Research conducted by the University of Manchester showed that people who have well-planned and organized schedules are more likely to achieve their goals than those who don't. The study emphasized the need for setting achievable goals, creating to-do lists, and allocating time for each task.

In addition, a study by the University of Nottingham found that using technology and tools such as time-tracking apps, calendars, and timers can significantly improve time management skills. The study also recommended the use of the Pomodoro technique, which involves breaking work into 25-minute intervals separated by short breaks, as an effective way to manage time.

The Pomodoro Technique is a time management method developed by Francesco Cirillo in the late 1980s. It is a simple yet effective technique that aims to improve focus, productivity, and time management by breaking work into short, focused intervals called "pomodoros."

The technique gets its name from the tomato-shaped kitchen timer, known as a "pomodoro" in Italian, that Cirillo used during his university days. Here's how the technique works:

- Set a specific task: Choose a task or project that you want to work on.
- Set the timer: Set a timer for 25 minutes, which is referred to as one "pomodoro." During this time, you dedicate yourself fully to working on the chosen task.
- Work without distractions: Focus solely on the task at hand, avoiding any distractions such as checking emails or social media.
- Take a short break: Once the timer goes off, take a short break of around 5 minutes. Use this time to relax, stretch, grab a drink, or do anything that helps you recharge.
- Repeat and track progress: After the short break, set the timer for another 25 minutes and continue working on the task. Repeat this process, taking short breaks after each pomodoro. After completing four consecutive pomodoros, take a longer break of about 15-30 minutes.

By breaking your work into these manageable intervals, the Pomodoro Technique helps maintain focus and prevents burnout. It also provides a structured approach to time management, allowing you to track your progress and estimate the time required for different tasks accurately.

While the technique is simple, it can be highly effective in boosting productivity and combating procrastination. It encourages you to work in concentrated bursts, promoting a sense of urgency and accomplishment. Additionally, the regular breaks prevent mental fatigue and improve overall productivity throughout the day.

The Pomodoro Technique is flexible and can be adapted to suit individual preferences. Some people find that shorter or longer pomodoro intervals work better for them, depending on the nature of their tasks or personal work style. The key is to find a rhythm that maximizes your focus and productivity while balancing it with regular breaks.

Whether you're studying, working on a project, or tackling a to-do list, incorporating the Pomodoro Technique into your workflow can help you manage your time effectively, enhance concentration, and achieve greater productivity.

As humans, we all have a desire to improve the quality of our lives. We work tirelessly day in and day out, in the hopes that tomorrow will be better than today. But what is the one constant that we all share, regardless of our status or wealth? Time. Time is the most precious resource we have, and once it's lost, it can never be regained. This is why effective time management is so crucial to our success.

Thankfully, nature has equipped us with the most complex organ on the planet - the human brain. Our brains are naturally wired to work with time and have an in-built mechanism for regulating the perception and processing of time. This mechanism is critical for effective time management.

The prefrontal cortex, the part of the brain responsible for planning, decision-making, and problem-solving, plays a crucial role in time management. It allows us to prioritize our tasks, allocate resources, and plan for the future. However, like any other muscle, our prefrontal cortex can become fatigued if we overwork it, which is why we need to learn to manage our time effectively.

When we successfully manage our time, our brains respond positively through the release of neurotransmitters like dopamine and serotonin, which provide a sense of accomplishment and motivation to continue managing our time effectively. This is why successful people often have excellent time management skills, and it's also why these skills are so critical to achieving our goals and improving our quality of life.

Mount Everest, the world's highest peak, is an example of an environment where time management can mean the difference between life and death.When climbing Mount Everest, climbers must acclimatize to the high altitude, which can take several weeks. During this time, they must carefully manage their time to ensure that they are physically and mentally ready to make the final push to the summit.

One example that highlights the critical role of time management in Everest climbing is the tragic event that unfolded in 1996. During that year, numerous commercial expeditions were striving to reach the summit of the majestic mountain. However, a formidable storm swept across the region, creating treacherous conditions for the climbers.

In the face of this unexpected and formidable challenge, time management became a matter of life and death. The storm's intensity and duration put the climbers at risk, as they were exposed to extreme cold, strong winds, and limited visibility. Those who had meticulously planned their ascent, factoring in weather conditions and ensuring adequate time for a safe return, were better equipped to handle the situation.

Unfortunately, not all climbers were able to effectively manage their time in this perilous environment. Some found themselves caught in the midst of the storm, unable to descend in time to seek shelter or safety. Tragically, lives were lost, and others faced harrowing experiences, enduring hours or even days of exposure to the elements.

Time management in Everest climbing is not merely about meeting schedules; it is a matter of survival. By being acutely aware of the time available and making informed decisions based on changing conditions, climbers can mitigate risks, avoid dangerous situations, and ensure their well-being.

The tragic events of 1996 on Everest serve as a poignant reminder of the critical role of time management in mountaineering, especially in such challenging environments. Climbers facing the formidable task of summiting Everest must diligently plan their ascent, taking into account factors such as weather forecasts, available daylight, and their own physical capabilities. Meticulous time management is essential for allocating sufficient time to reach the summit while also prioritizing a safe and timely descent. This tragedy underscores the vital importance of prioritizing safety and making well-informed decisions that align with the realities of the mountain environment. By practicing effective time management, climbers can significantly enhance their chances of a successful and safe expedition on the world's highest peak.

One factor that contributed to the disaster was poor time management. Some climbers had pushed themselves too hard to reach the summit, using up valuable energy and time that could have been used for the descent. Others had not turned back soon enough, even though they were running low on oxygen and other supplies.

In contrast, climbers who successfully summit Mount Everest often have excellent time management skills. They carefully plan their ascent and descent, taking into account factors such as weather conditions, available supplies, and their own physical condition. They pace themselves to conserve energy, taking breaks and sleeping at strategic points along the way. By doing so, they increase their chances of reaching the summit and returning safely.

The realm of space programs epitomizes the criticality of time management, where every second holds immense significance. The intricate nature of space missions necessitates meticulous attention to detail and flawless execution. With the potential for catastrophic consequences, even the slightest delay or mishap can have far-reaching impacts. Thus, time management becomes an indispensable aspect of planning and executing space programs at the most minute level.

Space programs demand an unparalleled level of precision, leaving no room for error or deviation from the established plan. The planning phase of these missions involves exhaustive calculations, simulations, and assessments to ensure the seamless functioning of every component. Each stage of the mission must be meticulously timed, with meticulous consideration given to various possible scenarios.

From launch windows to orbital maneuvers, time management plays a pivotal role in ensuring the success of space missions. Coordinating the activities of multiple spacecraft, ground stations, and mission control centers requires synchronizing operations with utmost precision. Even minor discrepancies in timing can disrupt intricate sequences of events, compromising the mission's objectives.

Additionally, unforeseen circumstances or emergencies demand rapid decision-making and adaptive time management. Space agencies must possess the agility to adjust plans and allocate resources efficiently in response to evolving situations. Time-sensitive tasks, such as crew safety protocols, system troubleshooting, or orbital adjustments, must be executed promptly to mitigate risks and ensure the mission's overall success.

In the unforgiving environment of space, time management is not simply a matter of productivity; it is a matter of survival and mission accomplishment. Each second is a valuable resource that must be leveraged optimally to maximize the mission's scientific outcomes, technological advancements, and the safety of astronauts.

By exemplifying unwavering commitment to meticulous time management, space programs showcase the dedication, expertise, and collaboration required to explore the vast unknown. Through the disciplined management of time, space agencies endeavor to unlock the mysteries of the universe while prioritizing the safety and success of their missions.

Effective time management is a proven strategy that not only enhances productivity but also reduces stress levels. When individuals practice efficient time management, they are more likely to achieve their goals and experience a greater sense of accomplishment.

One key aspect of time management is setting realistic goals and deadlines. By defining specific objectives and assigning appropriate timeframes, individuals can create a clear roadmap for their tasks and activities. This enables them to prioritize effectively, ensuring that important tasks receive adequate attention and are completed in a timely manner.

Moreover, tracking progress is an essential component of effective time management. Regularly monitoring and evaluating one's progress against set goals helps to identify areas that may require improvement or adjustment.

By prioritizing your tasks, breaking down big projects into smaller tasks, and tracking your progress, you'll be able to manage your time effectively and accomplish more in less time.

Discover the time management secrets of these highly successful and inspirational personalities who have mastered the art of balancing their personal and professional lives, although the list is by no means exhaustive, these honorable mentions are certainly worth emulating.

Narendra Modi: The Prime Minister of India, Narendra Modi is known for his excellent time management skills. He wakes up early and starts his day with yoga and meditation. He is known for his ability to work for long hours and is known to work 16 hours a day.

Ratan Tata: The former chairman of Tata Sons, Ratan Tata is known for his disciplined approach to time management. He is known to maintain a strict schedule and is always punctual for meetings.

Elon Musk:The founder of SpaceX and Tesla, Elon Musk, is known for his hectic schedule. He works 80-100 hours a week and sleeps just six hours a day. To manage his time, he divides his day into five-minute slots and sticks to a tight schedule. He has also been known to hold meetings while walking to save time.

Barack Obama: As the former President of the United States, Barack Obama had to manage a lot of responsibilities. To do this, he developed a habit of getting up early and working out before starting his day. He also prioritized his tasks and delegated work to his team whenever possible.

The concept of time management dates back to the early days of human history when people had a primitive understanding of time and how optimal timing was important for farming, hunting, and migration. Time management was a crucial aspect of the daily life of ancient civilizations. The oldest civilizations in the world, such as the Sumerians, Egyptians, and Indus Valley Civilization, developed sophisticated systems for measuring time and managing their daily lives. These systems were based on astronomical observations and the movements of the sun, moon, and stars.

The Sumerians, who lived in Mesopotamia (present-day Iraq) around 4000 BCE, used a sexagesimal (base-60) number system to measure time. They divided the day into 24 hours, each hour into 60 minutes, and each minute into 60 seconds. They also used a system of water clocks, called clepsydras, to measure the passage of time.

The Egyptians, who lived in the Nile Valley around 3000 BCE, used a system of 12 hours per day, with each hour varying in length depending on the time of year. They also divided the year into 12 months, based on the cycles of the moon. The Egyptians were famous for their use of sundials, which allowed them to track the movement of the sun and accurately determine the time of day.

The Indus Valley Civilization, which flourished in present-day in India and neighboring country around 2500 BCE, also used a lunar calendar, based on the cycles of the moon. They divided the day into eight parts, each corresponding to a different phase of the day. They also used a system of weights and measures, which helped them manage their resources and trade.

The Chinese used a lunisolar calendar, which combined the cycles of the moon and the sun. They divided the year into 12 months, each with 29 or 30 days, and added an extra month every few years to keep the calendar in sync with the seasons. They also used water clocks and sundials to measure time.

The Greeks used a variety of calendars, including the lunisolar calendar and the solar calendar. They also developed a system of dividing the day into 24 hours, which was based on the movement of the stars.

Overall, these ancient civilizations were highly effective in managing their time and resources, despite the limitations of their technology. By carefully observing the movements of the heavens, they were able to create sophisticated systems for measuring time and organizing their daily lives. These systems served as the foundation for many of the time management tools and techniques we still use today.

The Vedic period in India, which lasted from around 1500 BCE to 500 BCE, was a time of great intellectual and cultural growth. During this period, Vedic Indians developed a sophisticated understanding of time management, which was influenced by their religious beliefs and their knowledge of astronomy and mathematics. In this article, we will explore how Vedic Indians calculated time and managed their daily routines.

The Vedic Indians used a system of timekeeping that was based on the movements of the sun and the moon. They divided the day into 30 muhurtas, which were each about 48 minutes long. The muhurtas were further divided into praharas, which were about three hours long. There were eight praharas in a day, and each prahara had a specific name, such as pratah, sangava, and madhyahna.

In addition to the muhurtas and praharas, the Vedic Indians also used a system of lunar months to mark the passage of time. Each lunar month was divided into two pakshas, or phases of the moon. The waxing phase was called the shukla paksha, and the waning phase was called the krishna paksha. Each paksha was further divided into

15 tithis, which were about 24 hours long.

The Vedic Indians also had a sophisticated understanding of astronomy, which allowed them to calculate the movements of the planets and the stars. They used this knowledge to create a system of astrology, which they believed could be used to predict the future and guide their daily activities.

Based on their understanding of time and astrology, the Vedic Indians developed a system of daily routines that was designed to optimize their productivity and well-being. They believed that the best time to perform certain activities varied depending on the position of the planets and stars.

For example, they believed that the best time to study was during the morning hours, when the mind was most alert. They also believed that the best time to eat was during the midday hours, when the digestive system was most active. They believed that the evening hours were best for socializing and relaxation, and that the hours before bed were best for meditation and introspection.

The Vedic Indians were masters of time management, and their sophisticated understanding of time allowed them to live productive and fulfilling lives. While their methods may seem foreign to us today, their approach to time management can still offer valuable lessons for those seeking to optimize their daily routines and achieve their goals.

While these methods may seem rudimentary compared to modern time management techniques, they were highly effective for their time and allowed these civilizations to achieve great accomplishments in science, art, and architecture.

Throughout history, ancient civilizations recognized the importance of time and its management. They understood that time is a valuable resource that must be used wisely, and they developed methods for measuring and managing it effectively.

From the sundials of ancient Egypt to the water clocks of ancient Greece, these civilizations used a variety of tools and techniques to measure time. They observed the movements of the sun, moon, and stars, and used these observations to create calendars and clocks that allowed them to track the passage of days, months, and years.

Moreover, they also emphasized the importance of managing time effectively. They understood that time wasted is time lost forever and that productivity and efficiency were crucial to achieving their goals. For example, ancient Greeks believed that "kairos" or the right moment was crucial for success, and therefore, they placed great emphasis on taking advantage of opportunities as they arise.

Ancient civilizations also recognized the value of time in the larger scheme of life. They believed that the passage of time was part of a larger cycle of birth, growth, and decay, and that time must be used to achieve a higher purpose. For example, in Hinduism and Buddhism, time is seen as a tool for achieving enlightenment, and therefore, time management is essential in pursuing spiritual goals.

In conclusion, our ancient civilizations recognized the importance of time management, both for practical and spiritual reasons. They developed methods for measuring time and created systems for managing it effectively, and their insights continue to influence our understanding of time and productivity today.

ϼϼϼ

Let's look at the story of Brian and Harvey were two young boys who had been friends since childhood. They had grown up together, played together, and gone to school together. And when it was time for them to attend university, they decided to enroll in the same program and live in the same dormitory.

At first, everything was going smoothly. They were both passionate about computer science and worked hard to stay on top of their studies. But as the workload increased, they began to struggle with time management.

Brian would spend hours playing video games, leaving his assignments until the last minute. Harvey, on the other hand, would get lost in researching and analyzing topics, taking up all his time with studies and assignments. They soon realized that their poor time management skills were affecting their grades.

One day, after receiving poor marks on a group project, they decided that they needed to make a change. They went to the university's time management workshop and learned best practices, including making daily to-do lists, breaking down tasks into smaller pieces, and scheduling their time effectively.

Their efforts paid off, and they both graduated with honors. They landed jobs as developers in one of the prominent global companies, and they were thrilled. They continued to implement their time management skills in their jobs, and it helped them excel.

But it wasn't all smooth sailing. There were still times when they would slip up and procrastinate. One time, Brian got so distracted by a new video game that he forgot about an important deadline. And Harvey, on the other hand, would sometimes get lost in his work and forget to take breaks.

Despite these setbacks, they were able to laugh about it and support each other. They found that having a good sense of humor about their mistakes helped them stay motivated and positive.

Overall, Brian and Harvey learned that time management was a critical skill that they needed to master in order to succeed in their careers. And through their ups and downs, they learned to rely on each other and always find a reason to laugh.

ᗰᗰᗰ

Let's talk about John, a businessman who had to attend two crucial meetings in a different city. John had a habit of taking things as they come, and he never planned ahead. But little did he know that his habit would cause him to face difficulties in time management.

John woke up late and realized he had to rush to the airport. He skipped breakfast and grabbed a coffee on the way. On the flight, John planned to go through his presentations for the meetings, but he ended up watching a movie and taking a nap instead.

When John landed, he had to rush to his first meeting. Since he didn't have time to prepare, he went in unprepared. The meeting ended up running longer than expected as John had to put in extra effort to convince the customer.

Due to the longer meeting, John reached his second meeting late, which added to his troubles. Again, due to poor preparations, John's presentation went wrong, and he could not impress the client. Now exhausted from the two meetings, John met his long-time friend with low energy and enthusiasm.

John returned to the airport, feeling dejected and regretful for not planning ahead. If he had planned things in advance, he could have managed his time effectively and used it to win both clients and meet his friend with joy. But alas, he had to learn the hard way that planning ahead was the key to effective time management.

John was the kind of guy everyone liked at the office. He was always there to lend an ear, had great ideas, and worked hard. The only problem was that he couldn't manage his time to save his life.

Despite his colleagues' best efforts to remind him of deadlines and delegate tasks, John still struggled. He even missed a meeting with an important client once because he got distracted by a meme and spent the rest of the day sharing it with everyone in the office. Talk about a meme epidemic!

When John was put in charge of organizing the company's product launch event, everyone knew it was going to be a disaster. John procrastinated until the last minute, which didn't bode well for the event's success.

On the day of the launch, everything that could go wrong did. The invitations were disorganized, the registration page was a hot mess, and the food choices were a real gamble. It turns out, John had arranged the food just a day or two prior without even having a food tasting meeting with caterer, and let's just say, it wasn't the highlight of the event. Guests and clients were left wondering if they had accidentally stumbled into a bad catering nightmare.

But that wasn't the end of it. John's colleagues were so lost without him that they had to call him for everything, from setting up the sound system to projecting the product details on the screen. And if that wasn't bad enough, John had forgotten to invite a few important clients who ended up having to attend the event remotely. It was a complete disaster, and the investors were not impressed.

Despite his hard work, John missed out on a promotion because of the disaster product launch. It was a harsh lesson, but one that he needed to learn. If he had only managed his time better and delegated tasks effectively, the event could have been a huge success, and he could have achieved his goals.

John's transformation from a chaotic employee to a responsible worker wasn't an easy one. He had to make some serious changes in his habits, but he did it with humor and determination.

First, he decided to create a to-do list every day. But being John, he couldn't just write a plain old list. Instead, he created a fun game out of it. He wrote each task on a sticky note and arranged them in order of priority on his desk. Every time he finished a task, he would crumple up the sticky note and throw it into a small basketball hoop attached to his trash can. The sound of the crumpled paper hitting the basket was music to his ears.

Next, John knew he needed to set more realistic goals. Instead of aiming to complete an entire project in one day, he decided to break it down into smaller, more manageable tasks. He would treat each completed task as a mini-celebration, complete with a little dance party in his office.

John also started delegating tasks to his colleagues, but not before taking them out for coffee and donuts to butter them up. He found it easier to trust his coworkers with important tasks when they were all hyped up on sugar and caffeine.

To avoid multitasking, John would wear a funny hat that read "one task at a time" every time he needed to focus on a specific task. He knew it looked silly, but it helped him stay on track.

To avoid distractions, John started scheduling specific times to check his social media and memes. He would even set a timer for himself and race against the clock to see how many memes he could look at in five minutes.

John also knew the importance of taking breaks to avoid burnout, so he would take short walks around the office every hour. He would often bring a rubber chicken with him and make it squawk at unsuspecting coworkers.

Finally, John invested in some time management books and courses, but he found them all too boring. So, he decided to make his own time management course, complete with a PowerPoint presentation and a theme song that he would sing before every meeting.

Thanks to his humorous and unique approach to time management, John became a reliable and efficient employee, and even got promoted to a managerial position. And of course, he celebrated with a giant dance party in the break room.

In conclusion, time management is a crucial skill that can help us become more productive, efficient, and ultimately achieve our goals with ease. By implementing the strategies mentioned in this chapter, we can all improve our time management skills and enjoy a more balanced and fulfilling life.

To recap, here are some tips for efficient time management:

1. Make a to-do list and prioritize tasks based on their urgency and importance.
2. Set realistic goals and break down big projects into smaller, more manageable tasks.
3. Create a daily routine and stick to it.
4. Learn to delegate tasks when appropriate.
5. Take breaks throughout the day to recharge.
6. Avoid multitasking and focus on one task at a time.

7. Use technology tools such as calendars and reminders to keep track of deadlines and appointments.
8. Practice self-discipline and avoid distractions such as social media or unnecessary meetings.

Remember, time is a valuable resource that cannot be replenished. Therefore, it's important to use it wisely and make the most of every moment. With practice and determination, anyone can develop excellent time management skills and lead a more successful and fulfilling life.

ᐅᐅᐅ

Chapter Summary:

In this chapter, we delve into the significance of effective time management and explore various insights and studies on the subject. We discuss the metaphor of an empty jar and different-sized rocks, pebbles, sand, and water used by a music teacher to illustrate the importance of prioritizing tasks and making the most of limited time. The chapter highlights research conducted by universities, emphasizing the benefits of prioritizing tasks, minimizing distractions, setting achievable goals, and utilizing technology for time management. It stresses the importance of maintaining a well-planned and organized schedule and discusses the role of the prefrontal cortex in managing time effectively.

Furthermore, we examine examples from different fields where time management plays a critical role. The chapter showcases how climbers on Mount Everest and astronauts in space programs rely on effective time management for their safety and success. We also highlight individuals known for their exceptional time management skills, such as Narendra Modi, Ratan Tata, Elon Musk, and Barack Obama.

Taking a historical perspective, the chapter briefly explores how ancient civilizations, including the Sumerians, Egyptians, Indus Valley Civilization, and Vedic Indians, developed systems for measuring and managing time. Their understanding of the value of time and their use of different timekeeping methods and routines provide valuable insights.

Overall, the chapter emphasizes that time is a finite resource and effective time management is crucial for achieving success and improving the quality of life. It underscores the importance of prioritizing tasks, breaking down complex projects, minimizing distractions, setting realistic goals, leveraging technology and tools, and drawing inspiration from the time management practices of successful individuals.

Activity:

To help readers implement effective time management strategies in their own lives, a suggested activity is to create a personal time management plan. This activity can be done in the form of a written exercise or using a digital tool such as a spreadsheet or time management app. Here's a step-by-step guide for the activity:

1. *Assess your current time management habits: Take a moment to reflect on how you currently manage your time. Identify any challenges or areas where you feel you could improve.*

2. *Set clear goals and priorities: Define your short-term and long-term goals. Identify the tasks and activities that align with these goals and are of high priority. These are your "big rocks."*

3. *Create a schedule: Design a daily or weekly schedule that allocates specific time slots for your high-priority tasks. Consider your peak productivity times and allocate them for more challenging or important activities. Remember to include breaks and downtime to maintain a healthy work-life balance.*

4. *Break tasks into smaller steps: For larger projects or tasks, break them down into smaller, more manageable steps. This will make them less overwhelming and help you make progress consistently.*

5. *Minimize distractions: Identify common distractions that hinder your productivity, such as social media, emails, or noise. Implement strategies to minimize or eliminate these distractions during your dedicated work periods.*

6. *Utilize time management tools: Explore and select time management tools or techniques that resonate with you. These can include digital calendars, to-do lists, time-tracking apps, or the Pomodoro technique. Experiment with different tools and find what works best for you.*

7. *Monitor and adjust: Regularly review your time management plan to assess its effectiveness. Track your progress, identify any areas for improvement, and make adjustments as needed.*

8. *Seek accountability and support: Share your time management goals and progress with a friend, family member, or colleague. Having someone to hold you accountable can provide motivation and support in sticking to your plan.*

Furthermore, readers can also consider incorporating the following additional activities for effective time management:

1. *Time Tracking: Spend a week tracking how you spend your time. Use a journal or a time tracking app to record your activities throughout the day. This exercise will help you identify time-wasting activities or areas where you can optimize your schedule.*
2. *Prioritization Matrix: Create a prioritization matrix or a quadrant chart with two axes representing urgency and importance. Categorize your tasks accordingly to determine which ones require immediate attention and which ones can be delegated or postponed.*
3. *Time Blocking: Experiment with time blocking, a technique where you assign specific blocks of time for different activities or tasks. Dedicate focused time for specific projects, meetings, personal activities, or self-care. This approach can help maintain focus and prevent multitasking.*
4. *Delegation and Outsourcing: Identify tasks that can be delegated or outsourced to others. Whether it's at work or in personal life, delegating tasks to capable individuals can free up your time to focus on higher-priority activities.*
5. *Regular Review and Reflection: Set aside time at the end of each day, week, or month to review your time management practices. Reflect on what worked well and what could be improved. Make necessary adjustments to your schedule and strategies based on your observations.*
6. *Time Audit: Conduct a regular time audit to assess how you are spending your time. Evaluate whether your activities align with your priorities and goals. Adjust your schedule and allocate more time to activities that bring you closer to your desired outcomes.*

7. *Mindfulness and Self-Care: Incorporate mindfulness practices and self-care activities into your routine. Engaging in activities like meditation, exercise, or hobbies can enhance your focus, energy levels, and overall well-being, leading to improved productivity and time management.*

Remember, effective time management is a skill that requires practice and adaptation. Encourage readers to be patient with themselves and to make adjustments as needed. By incorporating these activities and strategies, readers can develop habits that optimize their time, increase productivity, and create a better work-life balance.

ϸϸϸ

TWO

Empowering Growth: Embrace Upskilling and Adaptation through Knowledge

❦

"Knowledge is power." - Sir Francis Bacon.

❧❧❧

Empowering growth is not just a one-time endeavor; it is a mindset that encompasses a lifelong commitment to continuous learning, upskilling, and adaptability. It is about recognizing the immense value of knowledge and its transformative potential. When we embrace the empowering growth mindset, we understand that knowledge is not static but a dynamic force that propels us forward. It fuels our curiosity, drives us to assess our skills and identify areas for improvement, and sets clear goals for upskilling. With this mindset, we actively seek out diverse learning opportunities, whether through online courses, workshops, or mentorship programs, to expand our knowledge base and acquire new skills.

The empowering growth mindset compels us to develop a thirst for learning and a willingness to adapt. We understand that change is inevitable, and we must be flexible and adaptable to navigate the ever-evolving landscape. By cultivating a learning mindset, we embrace challenges as opportunities for growth, learn from setbacks, and continuously pivot our skills and knowledge as needed. We understand that empowering growth is not about clinging to outdated methods but about embracing change, leveraging emerging trends, and staying ahead of the curve.

By adopting the empowering growth mindset, we unlock our potential for success. We leverage the knowledge and skills we have acquired through our upskilling journey to make a positive impact in our personal and professional endeavors. We become catalysts for change, seizing opportunities, and utilizing our expertise to achieve our goals. The empowering growth mindset empowers us to not only keep pace with the ever-changing world but also to thrive in it.

Reading and gaining knowledge play a pivotal role in both personal and professional growth. In the contemporary fast-paced world, where information is readily accessible, these activities have become more vital than ever. Regardless of whether you are a student, a professional, or an individual seeking personal development, reading offers invaluable benefits that can shape your outlook, expand your horizons, and keep you abreast of the latest advancements.

Reading serves as a gateway to new ideas, perspectives, and insights. It exposes us to a multitude of voices and experiences, enabling us to challenge our existing beliefs and broaden our understanding of the world. By engaging with diverse literature, whether it be books, articles, or research papers, we gain a deeper appreciation for different cultures, histories, and viewpoints. This exposure fosters empathy, critical thinking, and open-mindedness, nurturing our personal growth and facilitating meaningful connections with others.

Furthermore, reading is a powerful tool for upskilling and professional development. In an era of rapid technological advancements and evolving industries, staying current and relevant is essential. By immersing ourselves in educational and industry-specific literature, we acquire new knowledge, enhance our skills, and adapt to the changing demands of our fields. Reading allows us to explore emerging trends, gain insights from experts, and discover innovative approaches that can propel our careers forward.

Scientific research has also affirmed the positive impact of reading on brain development and overall well-being. Studies indicate that reading stimulates neural pathways, improves cognitive function, and enhances memory retention. Additionally, engaging with books and other reading materials has been shown to reduce stress, increase empathy, and improve overall mental well-being.

Incorporating reading into our daily routines can be a transformative practice. It cultivates a thirst for knowledge, ignites our imagination, and fosters a lifelong love of learning. Whether it is a few minutes dedicated to reading before bed or carving out dedicated time during the day, prioritizing reading allows us to invest in ourselves and unlock a world of possibilities.

According to the study conducted by the National Institute of Health, reading tend to increase neural connectivity in the brain and help to enhance cognitive functions such as attention, reasoning and memory. Reading and learning from various sources is life essentials to stop from getting stagnated, reading exposes us to broad set of ideas, perspectives and cultures, it helps us to broaden our understanding of the world, helps to emphasize with people from different background and cultures.

Making informed decisions can only happen when you possess information about things and subjects, critical thinking is essential for todays leaders to make rational decisions. In a world where we are constantly bombarded with information, making informed decisions is more important than ever. Without access to the right information, we risk making decisions that are not in our best interest. This is where critical thinking comes into play. It enables us to analyze, evaluate, and interpret information in order to make rational and informed decisions.

For leaders, critical thinking is especially important. The decisions they make can have a significant impact on their organizations and the people they serve. By being able to think critically, leaders can avoid making hasty decisions based on incomplete or inaccurate information. They can also consider multiple perspectives and potential outcomes before making a final decision. As individuals, making wise decisions is also crucial. From financial investments to everyday purchases, the decisions we make can have long-lasting effects on our lives. By acquiring the right information and applying critical thinking, we can make decisions that align with our values and goals.

On the other hand, if we don't take the time to learn and acquire new information, we run the risk of being misled or making uninformed decisions. This can lead to missed opportunities, wasted resources, and even negative consequences. Without critical thinking, we may be more susceptible to manipulation, bias, and false information. Reading can also help us develop a sense of confidence and self-esteem, it naturally provides a sense of pride and accomplishment in our abilities while also improving our creativity to think differently, explore new ideas and imagine other possibilities, which is very important in solving problems. Reading not only expands your knowledge but also improves your social relationships. When you have a diverse range of topics to discuss with people from different backgrounds and cultures, it creates a sense of interest and respect towards you. You become a person with a great depth of knowledge, and people start relying on you for advice and guidance. In the professional world, this becomes even more crucial. You need to convince your boss or team about a plan, or you need to close a deal with a potential client, and that's when your knowledge and confidence come into play. With reading, you gain critical thinking skills, problem-solving abilities, and the capability to provide solutions in multiple ways. Your professional success relies on your ability to make informed decisions, and reading helps you achieve that. You become more confident in your work, and people around you trust you more. You become a valuable asset to your team or organization, and your career graph keeps soaring.

On the other hand, people who don't read or learn new things often lack the confidence and skills required to succeed. They may struggle to make informed decisions and may have to rely on others to guide them. This can lead to missed opportunities, wrong investments, and overall lack of growth in life. There have been numerous studies on the benefits of reading and studying. One study conducted by the University of Sussex found that just six minutes of reading can reduce stress levels by 68%. Another study published in the journal Social Science & Medicine found that people who read books regularly live longer than those who don't read at all. Furthermore, a study conducted by the University of California, Berkeley found that reading can improve empathy and emotional intelligence, which can lead to better relationships with others.

In the military, reading, learning, and adapting are not just important; they are a matter of life and death. Knowledge is power, and military personnel must constantly strive to expand their understanding and skills to navigate the complexities of their profession successfully. Reading and learning provide them with the essential knowledge and insights needed to excel in combat situations.

For military personnel, staying informed and continuously learning is crucial to their effectiveness and survival. They must study and understand the latest advancements in weaponry, equipment, and tactics to gain an edge on the battlefield. By reading military literature, historical accounts, and strategic analyses, they can learn from past experiences and apply that knowledge to present situations.

Moreover, military personnel must adapt swiftly and effectively to changing circumstances. In the chaos of combat, the ability to analyze evolving situations, make critical decisions, and adjust strategies on the fly is paramount. Reading and learning contribute to their adaptability by providing a broader understanding of military operations, leadership principles, and problem-solving techniques. Armed with this knowledge, they can assess risks, devise innovative approaches, and respond appropriately to unforeseen challenges.

Failure to read, learn, and adapt in the military can have dire consequences. Ignorance or resistance to change can lead to poor decision-making, inadequate preparation, and ultimately, failure in mission objectives. In combat, this could result in unnecessary casualties, lost battles, or even the defeat of an entire campaign.

Therefore, military personnel understand that reading, learning, and adapting are not optional but necessary for their personal and professional growth. By continuously expanding their knowledge base, embracing new ideas, and remaining open to learning, they can enhance their skills, leadership capabilities, and overall effectiveness. This commitment to growth and adaptation ensures they are better equipped to face the ever-changing and unpredictable nature of their profession.

For example, during the Vietnam War, American forces struggled with the Viet Cong's guerrilla warfare tactics. The Viet Cong often used booby traps and other unconventional methods to attack American troops, who were trained in conventional warfare tactics. The American military was slow to adapt and learn from their mistakes, resulting in unnecessary casualties. However, after recognizing the need to learn and adapt, the American military began to develop new tactics and strategies to counter the Viet Cong's tactics. One such strategy was the creation of specialized units, such as the tunnel rats, who were trained to navigate and clear the underground tunnel systems that the Viet Cong used to hide and move around undetected. In addition, the military also began to prioritize language training and cultural understanding, recognizing the importance of understanding the local population and customs to gain their support and cooperation. Overall, the Vietnam War serves as a stark reminder of the importance of learning and adapting in the military. Failure to do so can have dire consequences, while a commitment to continuous learning and improvement can save lives and ensure mission success.

ᐅᐅᐅ

Let's analyze the story of Brian and Harvey, Brian and Harvey both started their new jobs in a software development company on the same day. They were assigned to work on the same project, and their manager was impressed with their work. However, their paths started to diverge after a few weeks. Brian spent his evenings and weekends reading about the latest trends in the software industry, learning new programming languages, and improving his technical skills. He also read about business strategy, communication, and management.

On the other hand, Harvey preferred to spend his free time watching TV, playing video games, and hanging out with his friends. As the project progressed, Brian started to make valuable contributions, providing creative solutions to complex problems, suggesting improvements, and communicating effectively with the team. He was confident and always willing to take on new challenges. Harvey, on the other hand, struggled to keep up with the pace of the project. He lacked creativity and critical thinking skills, and his communication with the team was often unclear and ineffective.

One day, the team encountered a critical issue that needed urgent attention. The manager asked both Brian and Harvey to come up with solutions. Brian quickly analyzed the situation, used his critical thinking skills to identify the root cause, and proposed a well-thought-out solution. Harvey, however, struggled to understand the problem and came up with a vague and ineffective solution. The manager was impressed with Brian's abilities and offered him a promotion to a leadership position in the team. Harvey, unfortunately, was let go due to his lack of skills and poor performance.

Brian's dedication to learning and improving his skills had paid off, and he was now on the path to success. Harvey, on the other hand, had missed out on the opportunity due to his lack of effort and unwillingness to learn. This story highlights the importance of reading and learning in the professional world. In today's fast-paced and ever-changing environment, continuous learning is essential to stay relevant and competitive. Those who invest time and effort in improving their skills and knowledge are more likely to succeed and advance in their careers.

ᗡᗡᗡ

When companies fail to adapt to changing circumstances, they face a range of potential consequences that can significantly impact their success and survival in the business world. Here are some common outcomes of not embracing adaptation.

Nokia was a market leader in the mobile phone industry. Their phones were reliable, durable, and had a loyal customer base. However, as technology advanced, Nokia failed to keep up with the changing times. At the turn of the millennium, the smartphone revolution began. Companies like Apple and Samsung introduced phones that were more than just communication devices, but rather, personal computers in the palm of your hand. These phones had touchscreens, app stores, and were fully integrated with the internet. But Nokia didn't see the value in this new technology. They believed that their loyal customers would always want a traditional keypad phone, and so they continued to produce the same types of phones they always had. They failed to see that the world was changing, and that people wanted more from their phones than just making calls and sending texts. By the time Nokia realized their mistake, it was too late. They tried to catch up by releasing smartphones of their own, but they were already years behind the competition. They were also slow to adapt to the new trend of app stores and mobile internet, which left them struggling to keep up with the likes of Apple and Samsung.

In 2013, Nokia was acquired by Microsoft, and the once-great phone company faded into obscurity. All because they failed to learn and adapt to the changing times. The story of Nokia is a cautionary tale for any business or individual who thinks that they can continue to operate the same way they always have. In today's rapidly changing world, it's essential to keep learning, growing, and adapting to stay relevant and competitive.

Why is reading important? Reading is an excellent way to gain knowledge and expand your vocabulary. It helps you develop critical thinking skills, improves your memory and concentration, and enhances your communication skills. Reading also helps reduce stress and can be a great way to relax and unwind after a long day.

How to make reading a habit? Making reading a habit can be challenging, but with a few simple strategies, it can be achieved. Set aside a specific time each day for reading, even if it's just for 15 minutes. Create a reading list of books or articles that interest you, and keep them accessible in your bag or on your phone. Join a book club or reading group to motivate yourself and share your thoughts and ideas with others.

Many successful people, from Bill Gates to Oprah Winfrey, attribute their success to reading and gaining knowledge. Warren Buffet, one of the world's richest men, spends up to 80% of his day reading. Elon Musk, the CEO of Tesla and SpaceX, has stated that he learned how to build rockets by reading books. J.K. Rowling, the author of the Harry Potter series, has stated that she reads constantly to improve her writing skills.

Reading is a powerful tool that can help you achieve personal and professional growth. By making reading a habit, you can broaden your horizons, challenge your perspectives, and stay up-to-date with the latest trends and developments in your field. So, start reading today and unlock the power of knowledge.

Reading is undoubtedly a valuable source of knowledge and inspiration. It opens up a world of ideas, insights, and perspectives that can transform our lives. However, the true value of reading lies not just in the act of absorbing information, but in the implementation of what we have learned. Without applying what we read, all the wisdom and knowledge we acquire remain dormant, rendering our reading efforts futile.

Imagine a scenario where you read numerous books on personal development, productivity, or goal-setting, but fail to take action on the principles and strategies outlined within them. In such a case, reading becomes a passive exercise, providing temporary motivation or intellectual stimulation, but lacking the transformative power that comes from putting knowledge into practice.

To capitalize on the benefits of reading, we must bridge the gap between theory and action. It is through implementation that we truly internalize and benefit from what we have read. Implementation involves taking the ideas, concepts, and strategies we encounter in books and actively incorporating them into our lives. It requires deliberate effort, discipline, and a commitment to personal growth.

Implementing what we read allows us to test theories, experiment with new approaches, and discover what works best for us. It is through this hands-on experience that we gain a deeper understanding of the concepts we have encountered. We may stumble and encounter challenges along the way, but it is through these practical experiences that we refine our understanding and develop the skills necessary for personal and professional growth.

Moreover, implementation fuels momentum. When we take consistent action based on what we have learned, we build momentum towards our goals. Each step forward, no matter how small, contributes to progress and propels us closer to success. By consistently implementing the ideas we have gained from our reading, we transform knowledge into tangible results.

Implementing what we read also fosters accountability. When we put our knowledge into action, we hold ourselves accountable for our growth and development. It shifts our focus from passive consumption to active participation in our own transformation. We become responsible for the outcomes we desire, and through implementation, we take ownership of our success.

Additionally, implementation breeds creativity and innovation. As we apply what we have learned, we begin to adapt and customize strategies to suit our unique circumstances. We learn to think critically, problem-solve, and develop our own ideas. The process of implementation becomes a fertile ground for innovation, allowing us to explore new possibilities and uncover untapped potential.

Reading is an essential part of personal and professional development. It provides us with knowledge, insights, and inspiration. However, the true value of reading lies in the implementation of what we have learned. By actively applying the concepts, strategies, and ideas encountered in books, we unlock the transformative power of reading. Implementation propels us towards growth, accountability, creativity, and ultimately, the achievement of our goals. So, as you read and absorb knowledge, remember to take intentional steps to implement what you have learned. Embrace the journey of putting ideas into action, and watch as your reading becomes a catalyst for positive change and extraordinary results.

Meet John, a passionate entrepreneur who dreams of launching his own successful startup. He spends hours every week devouring books on entrepreneurship, innovation, and business strategy. John is captivated by the stories of renowned entrepreneurs who have achieved remarkable success through their innovative ideas.

One day, while browsing a bookstore, John stumbles upon a book titled "The Lean Startup Method: Building a Business with Speed and Agility." Intrigued by the promise of a systematic approach to launching a startup, John eagerly dives into its pages. The book introduces concepts such as minimum viable product (MVP), rapid experimentation, and customer feedback loops.

As John reads, his mind starts buzzing with ideas. He envisions himself building a lean and agile startup, where every decision is backed by data and validated by real customer feedback. The book has ignited his entrepreneurial spirit and sparked a desire to put these concepts into practice.

However, as time goes by, John realizes that he has fallen into a familiar trap. He continues to read more books on entrepreneurship, attending seminars, and consuming podcasts, but struggles to translate the knowledge into tangible action. The ideas remain confined within the pages of the books, while his dream of launching a successful startup remains unfulfilled.

Determined to break free from this cycle of passive learning, John decides to take a different approach. He recognizes that knowledge without action is merely an illusion of progress. With a renewed sense of purpose, John sets out to implement the principles he has learned, guided by the teachings of "The Lean Startup Method."

John begins by identifying a problem he wants to solve through his startup. He conducts market research and interviews potential customers to gain a deep understanding of their pain points and needs. Armed with this knowledge, he starts building a minimum viable product—a stripped down version of his idea that allows him to test the market demand and gather real-world feedback.

Embracing the iterative nature of the lean startup methodology, John launches his MVP and actively seeks feedback from early adopters. He carefully listens to their suggestions and uses their input to refine and improve his product. With each iteration, John gets closer to building a solution that truly addresses the customers' needs.

Along the way, John faces numerous challenges and setbacks. However, armed with the principles he learned from the book, he approaches these obstacles as learning opportunities. He embraces failure as a necessary part of the entrepreneurial journey and adjusts his strategy accordingly. Through persistent experimentation and adaptation, John starts gaining traction and attracting a growing user base.

As John's startup gains momentum, he realizes the true power of implementing what he has learned. The book he once read becomes more than a source of inspiration—it becomes his playbook for success. He constantly refers back to its teachings, leveraging its insights to make informed decisions, pivot when necessary, and scale his business.

Through his commitment to implementation, John experiences firsthand the transformative power of combining knowledge with action. His startup gains recognition in the industry, attracting the attention of investors and strategic partners. What started as a dream is now a thriving venture, making a positive impact on the lives of its customers.

John's story serves as a reminder that implementing what we read is the key to unlocking the true potential of knowledge. Like John, each of us can harness the wisdom and ideas we encounter in books to drive meaningful change in our lives. By taking intentional steps, applying what we learn, and persistently pushing forward, we can turn our dreams into reality and achieve extraordinary success.

As you reflect on your own reading journey, consider how you can follow in John's footsteps. How can you apply the principles and strategies you learn from books in your own pursuits? What specific actions can you take to implement the lessons and insights you encounter?

Remember, it is through consistent action that the seeds of knowledge blossom into tangible results. Take a moment to consider your own aspirations and the books you have read. How can you translate the concepts and ideas into practical steps that propel you toward your goals?

Perhaps you've read books on personal finance, learning about budgeting, saving, and investing. How can you implement these principles in your own life? Can you create a budgeting system, set up automatic savings, or explore investment opportunities? By taking deliberate action, you can transform your financial well-being.

Or maybe you've delved into books on health and fitness, discovering strategies for exercise, nutrition, and overall well-being. How can you incorporate these principles into your daily routine? Can you develop a workout plan, experiment with healthy recipes, or practice mindfulness exercises? By putting these ideas into practice, you can improve your physical and mental health.

The key is to bridge the gap between theory and action. It's not enough to passively consume information; you must actively engage with it. Start by setting clear goals related to what you have learned. Break down these goals into actionable steps, creating a roadmap for implementation.

Hold yourself accountable by establishing routines and habits that support your progress. Create reminders, track your actions, and celebrate milestones along the way. Engage in reflection and self-assessment to identify areas of improvement and adjust your approach as needed.

Remember that implementation is not always smooth sailing. There will be obstacles, setbacks, and moments of self-doubt. But it is through these challenges that you will grow, learn, and develop resilience. Embrace the journey as an opportunity for growth and self-discovery.

Seek support from others who share your goals or have expertise in the areas you're pursuing. Engage in conversations, join communities, or seek out mentors who can provide guidance and encouragement. Collaboration and accountability can enhance your implementation efforts and accelerate your progress.

Ultimately, the true value of reading lies in its ability to inspire and inform action. As you embark on your journey of implementation, you will discover the immense satisfaction and fulfillment that come from turning knowledge into tangible results. Your reading experiences will become catalysts for personal and professional growth.

So, as you close the pages of each book, ask yourself: How can I take what I have learned and put it into practice? How can I transform these ideas into actions that lead me closer to my goals? The power to implement what you read lies within you. Embrace it, and watch as your life becomes a reflection of the wisdom you have gained.

Conclusion: Reading is undeniably important, but it's equally crucial to bridge the gap between theory and reality by implementing what you read. Knowledge alone has limited value; it is in the application of that knowledge where true growth and success are found. So, as you continue your reading journey, remember to take intentional steps towards implementing what you learn, for it is through action that you can transform your life and capitalize on the wisdom gained from the pages of books.

ᛩᛩᛩ

Chapter Summary:

In this chapter, we explored the power of the empowering growth mindset and the role it plays in personal and professional development. We emphasized the importance of adopting a mindset that embraces continuous learning, upskilling, and adaptability as the key drivers of success.

Throughout the chapter, we discussed the transformative nature of the empowering growth mindset. We recognized that knowledge is not static but a dynamic force that propels us forward. By actively seeking diverse learning opportunities, such as online courses, workshops, and mentorship programs, we expanded our knowledge base and acquired new skills.

We also delved into the significance of reading as a tool for knowledge acquisition and personal growth. Through active reading, we engaged with the text, annotated, summarized, and questioned, maximizing our learning potential. Reading opened doors to new ideas, perspectives, and experiences, broadening our horizons and deepening our understanding.

Implementing what we learned was another crucial aspect of the empowering growth mindset. By applying our acquired knowledge and skills in practical ways, we solidified our understanding and made a tangible impact. Whether through utilizing our expertise in challenging projects or sharing our insights with others, we actively implemented and embraced growth.

Activity:

Empowering a growth mindset involves upskilling, gaining knowledge, reading, and adapting. Here is an activity one could follow to empower a growth mindset:

1. *Reflection and Implementation: After completing each book or article, take time to reflect on the insights gained and how they relate to your goals and aspirations. Consider how you can implement the newfound knowledge and skills in your personal and professional life.*
2. *Journaling: Maintain a journal specifically dedicated to your empowering growth journey. Write reflections, insights, and action plans based on what you have learned. Track your progress, challenges faced, and milestones achieved.*
3. *Implementing and Practicing: Actively implement what you have learned in real-life situations. Apply the new knowledge and skills to your work, projects, or interactions with others. Experiment with different strategies and techniques to see what works best for you.*
4. *Seeking Feedback and Support: Share your progress and insights with trusted friends, colleagues, or mentors. Seek their feedback and support in implementing your new knowledge and skills. Engage in discussions to deepen your understanding and gain different perspectives.*
5. *Continuous Learning: Keep building your reading list and exploring new topics to continue your empowering growth journey. Embrace the mindset of lifelong learning, consistently seeking opportunities to expand your knowledge and skills.*

Remember, the key to this activity is not just reading for the sake of reading but actively engaging with the material, reflecting on its relevance to your goals, and implementing what you learn. By incorporating these practices into your routine, you can foster an empowering growth mindset and embark on a transformative journey of personal and professional development.

❧❧❧

THREE

The Networking Edge: Supercharge Your Success through Connections

"Success in business is all about making connections. It's about personal contact. You need to get out and about, whether that's meeting clients, attending conferences or visiting suppliers. And you need to be on the lookout for opportunities." - Richard Branson.

ᐅᐅᐅ

In ancient times, humans were master networkers without even needing Wi-Fi or a LinkedIn account. They knew the true meaning of connection—meeting face-to-face, sharing stories around the fire, and collaborating on mammoth-hunting strategies. But alas, fast forward to the modern era, and our networking skills have seemingly taken a nosedive into the abyss of virtual platforms and superficial connections. We now live in a world where we boast hundreds, if not thousands, of "friends" online. But let's be honest, how many of those friends would actually lend us a hand in times of real trouble? Probably as many as the number of times we've won the lottery. It seems we've become experts at collecting virtual buddies like Pokémon cards, yet we struggle to find someone who can lend a listening ear or offer genuine support.

Our modern-day networks have transformed into a bizarre virtual circus. We scroll through an endless stream of selfies, food pictures, and political rants, occasionally leaving a digital thumbs-up or a generic comment like "Great pic!" as if we were art critics. We've perfected the art of superficiality, spending hours curating the perfect online persona while neglecting the real human connections that truly matter. The irony is that we're more "connected" than ever, yet we're lonelier than a penguin in the Sahara.

We attend networking events where people exchange business cards as if they were playing a game of collectible trading cards. We connect on platforms with catchy names like "FriendFace" or "InstaGlam," where our self-worth is determined by the number of followers we have, rather than the depth of our relationships. But fear not! There is hope for us lost souls in the digital abyss. We can reclaim the lost art of networking and transform it from a soulless numbers game into a meaningful and impactful practice. It starts by breaking free from the shackles of our screens and embracing genuine human interaction. Let's dust off our social skills and engage in real conversations, where we listen more than we speak, and seek to understand rather than to impress.

Remember, networking is not just about swapping business cards or collecting "likes" on a selfie. It's about forging authentic connections, nurturing relationships, and offering support to others without expecting an immediate return. So, put down your virtual pet and step out into the real world. Engage in conversations, join communities, and be present for the people around you. Embrace the beauty of networking beyond the pixelated realm, and you'll discover a world of meaningful connections that can truly enrich your life. In this digital age, let's show the world that we're more than just avatars and status updates. Let's be the generation that brings back the lost art of networking, one genuine connection at a time. And hey, who knows, maybe we'll even catch a mammoth or two along the way!

Networking is the art of building relationships with people who can help you achieve your goals. Whether you're looking for new business opportunities, seeking career advice, or trying to expand your knowledge and skills, having the right network can make all the difference. In this chapter, we'll explore the importance of networking, how to build a strong network, and how to leverage it for success.

Time management and continuous learning by reading are essential skills to succeed in life, but they are not enough. To truly excel, you need to have a solid network of people around you who can support you and help you grow. Having a strong network of individuals who share your values and goals is critical for your success.

Building your network is not just about collecting business cards or LinkedIn connections. It's about cultivating genuine relationships with people who are willing to support you, offer feedback, and help you when you need it the most. These people can be your mentors, colleagues, friends, or even family members. They are the ones who can provide guidance and advice, offer emotional support, and connect you to other people who can help you achieve your goals.

The key to building a great network is to choose the right people to be a part of it. Surrounding yourself with negative, toxic, or unsupportive individuals can hold you back and prevent you from achieving your full potential. Therefore, it's crucial to be selective when choosing the people, you spend your time with.

Take the time to reflect on your goals and values and identify the people who share them. Seek out individuals who are passionate about the same things as you and who are willing to support your journey. Look for people who are positive, motivated, and have a growth mindset.

When you find the right people, invest time and effort into building meaningful relationships with them. Attend events, participate in discussions, and be open to feedback and advice. Take the initiative to connect with people and offer value to them. Remember that building a network is a two-way street, and you need to be willing to give as much as you receive.

Your network can define your destiny. The people you surround yourself with can shape your beliefs, habits, and attitudes. They can inspire you, challenge you, and help you overcome obstacles. Having a strong network can give you the confidence and support you need to take risks, pursue your dreams, and achieve success.

There are several examples of birds and animals that rely on building strong networks and social structures within their communities. Here are a few notable examples:

Dolphins: Dolphins are highly social creatures known for their complex social networks. They live in groups called pods and maintain strong bonds within their pod members. These networks are crucial for hunting, protection against predators, and navigating their marine environment. Dolphins communicate with one another using a variety of vocalizations, which helps them coordinate group activities and stay connected within their network.

Elephants: Elephants are highly intelligent and social animals that live in tight-knit family groups called herds. Within these herds, they form strong social bonds and establish a hierarchical structure led by the oldest and most experienced female, known as the matriarch. Elephants rely on their social network for cooperation, protection, and sharing resources such as knowledge of water sources and migration routes.

Ants: Ants are renowned for their complex social networks and highly organized colonies. They work together in a coordinated manner, dividing tasks and communicating through pheromones. Ants establish intricate networks for foraging, defense, and resource allocation, ensuring the survival and prosperity of the entire colony.

Honeybees: Honeybees are known for their remarkable ability to work together in highly organized colonies. They communicate through intricate dance patterns and pheromones to relay information about food sources and potential nesting sites. Honeybees rely on their network to efficiently gather nectar and pollen, maintain the hive, and ensure the survival of the entire colony.

Wolves: Wolves are highly social animals that live in packs, forming strong family bonds. They collaborate in hunting, raising their young, and defending their territory. Wolves rely on their network to communicate and coordinate their efforts, maximizing their chances of success during hunts and ensuring the survival of the pack.

In all of these examples, building strong networks and social structures within their respective communities is crucial for these birds and animals' survival, protection, and overall well-being. These networks facilitate cooperation, information sharing, and division of labor, ultimately increasing their chances of success in various aspects of their lives.

Why Networking is Important

In today's fast-paced and ever-changing world, networking is more critical than ever before. It's not just about who you know, but about the knowledge and resources that they can provide you with. A strong network can be a valuable source of information and insights that can help you stay ahead of the competition and make informed decisions.

Your network can also be a powerful tool for building your reputation and credibility. By connecting with like-minded individuals and sharing your knowledge and skills, you can establish yourself as a thought leader in your field. Your network can help you showcase your expertise, highlight your achievements, and gain recognition for your contributions.

But networking is not just about what you can get; it's also about what you can give. By sharing your knowledge and resources with others, you can build trust and establish meaningful relationships. Your network can help you expand your knowledge and skills, learn from others, and discover new opportunities for growth and development.

In today's competitive world, networking is no longer a luxury but a necessity. It's a skill that everyone needs to master if they want to succeed. By investing time and effort into building and nurturing your network, you can gain a competitive advantage, expand your knowledge and skills, and create new opportunities for growth and development. So, start building your network today and see how it can help you achieve your goals and unlock your full potential.

Identify your goals: Before you start networking, it's important to identify your goals. What do you want to achieve? Who do you need to connect with to achieve your goals?

A strong network can provide individuals with a multitude of benefits and opportunities that can enhance their personal and professional lives in numerous ways such as:

1. Access to Opportunities: A strong network provides access to a wide range of opportunities. Whether it's job openings, business partnerships, or collaborative

projects, your network can be a valuable source of information and connections. Through networking, you can tap into opportunities that may not be readily available through other channels.

2. Knowledge and Insights: Your network consists of individuals with diverse backgrounds, experiences, and expertise. By connecting with them, you gain access to a wealth of knowledge and insights. Networking allows you to learn from others, exchange ideas, and stay up-to-date with the latest industry trends. This knowledge can help you make informed decisions and stay ahead in your field.

3. Support and Advice: Building a strong network means surrounding yourself with a supportive community. Your network can offer guidance, advice, and mentorship. When faced with challenges or uncertainties, you can turn to your network for support and insights from those who have been through similar situations. Having a reliable support system can boost your confidence and help you navigate obstacles more effectively.

4. Collaboration and Partnerships: Networking opens doors to potential collaborations and partnerships. By connecting with individuals who share similar interests or complementary skills, you can explore joint ventures, co-create projects, or expand your business reach. Collaboration can lead to mutual growth and increased opportunities for both parties involved.

5. Personal and Professional Growth: Your network influences your personal and professional growth. Surrounding yourself with motivated and ambitious individuals can inspire and challenge you to strive for greater achievements. Through networking, you can

learn from the successes and failures of others, gain new perspectives, and expand your horizons. Your network can serve as a source of inspiration, motivation, and accountability.

6. Increased Visibility and Influence: Building a strong network helps increase your visibility within your industry or professional community. When you actively engage with others and contribute value, you become known for your expertise and reputation. This visibility can lead to opportunities for speaking engagements, leadership roles, and becoming a trusted authority in your field. With an influential network, you can make a positive impact and inspire others.

ᚦᚦᚦ

Remember Brian and Harvey, wherein Brian was quick learner and invested time on learning, while Harvey soon realized that he had made a mistake. He saw his friend Brian achieve great success, and he realized that he had fallen behind. He knew that he needed to catch up if he wanted to advance in his career. Harvey started investing time and effort into learning new skills and developing his knowledge just like his friend Brian, but Harvey also started networking with his colleagues and attending industry events.

Harvey's realization that he had been neglecting the power of networking was a turning point in his career. As he started attending industry events and building relationships with his colleagues, he began to see the benefits of having a strong network.

Harvey's networking skills were exceptional. He was able to build rapport with his colleagues, and he was genuinely interested in their work and perspectives. He also took the initiative to reach out to others in his field, which helped him to gain new knowledge and insights.

As Harvey's network grew, so did his opportunities. He was invited to participate in new projects and collaborate with other teams. He was also able to leverage his relationships to gain exposure and recognition for his work.

Harvey's ability to connect with others and build strong relationships gave him a competitive edge. He was able to tap into his network to gain new ideas and approaches to solving problems, which helped him to become a more effective and efficient developer.

Ultimately, it was Harvey's networking skills that helped him to surpass Brian in terms of success and achievements. By investing time and effort into building relationships and expanding his network, he was able to gain a new level of fulfillment in his career.

Harvey's story is a testament to the power of networking in today's fast-paced and competitive world. By building strong relationships with colleagues and industry peers, you can gain valuable insights and opportunities that can help you achieve success and fulfillment in your career.

ᗁᗁᗁ

The first step to leveraging your network is to identify your personal and professional goals. What do you want to achieve in your career or personal life? Once you have a clear understanding of your goals, you can start to build relationships with people who can help you achieve them. This could include mentors, colleagues, industry experts, or even friends and family.

However, it's important to approach networking with the right mindset. Networking is not about using people to get what you want. It's about building mutually beneficial relationships where both parties can help each other. To do this, you need to be honest and transparent about your intentions. Don't just reach out to people when you need something. Instead, focus on building genuine connections based on common interests, values, and goals.

One way to contribute to your network is to share your knowledge and expertise. If you have a particular skill or area of expertise, offer to help others who may be struggling in that area. Share articles, resources, or insights that could be helpful. By doing this, you are not only building your reputation as an expert in your field, but you are also building trust and credibility with your network.

Another way to contribute to your network is to introduce people to each other. If you know two people who could benefit from each other's expertise, make an introduction. This is a great way to add value to your network while also building relationships between others. By doing this, you are also demonstrating your willingness to help others, which can lead to more opportunities for you in the future.

It's important to remember that networking is a long-term strategy. Building strong relationships takes time and effort, but the benefits can be immense. By contributing honestly and without thinking of personal gain, you can build a strong network of people who will be there to support you throughout your career and personal life.

One real-life example of how networking helped an individual grow in their career and succeed is the story of Sheryl Sandberg, the Chief Operating Officer (COO) of Facebook.

In her early career, Sandberg worked as the Chief of Staff for the United States Secretary of the Treasury and then as the Vice President of Global Online Sales and

Operations at Google. However, despite her impressive qualifications and experience, she faced significant challenges when she tried to negotiate for her salary and position at Google.

Sandberg turned to her mentor, former Google CEO Eric Schmidt, for advice. Schmidt encouraged her to "sit at the table," to speak up and make her voice heard, and to build a network of supporters who could help her achieve her goals.

Following Schmidt's advice, Sandberg became more vocal and active in her networking efforts, attending industry events and building relationships with other influential leaders in the tech industry. This networking paid off when she was recruited by Mark Zuckerberg to become the COO of Facebook in 2008.

At Facebook, Sandberg continued to leverage her networking skills to drive the company's growth and success. She built strong relationships with key advertisers, investors, and partners, and used her network to stay up-to-date on the latest industry trends and innovations.

Sandberg's story is a powerful example of how networking can be a key driver of career success. By building relationships with the right people and leveraging those relationships to gain insights, feedback, and opportunities, individuals can achieve their goals and thrive in their careers.

Leveraging Your Network for Success

Once you have built a strong network, it's important to leverage it for success. Here are some ways to do this:

1. Get market information: Use your network to gather information about the latest trends, innovations, and challenges in your field.
2. Seek feedback: Use your network to get feedback on your ideas, products, or services. This can help you refine your approach and improve your results.
3. Learn and grow: Use your network to learn from others and expand your knowledge and skills. Attend workshops, webinars, and training sessions to stay up-to-date with the latest developments in your field.
4. Create opportunities: Use your network to create new business opportunities, partnerships, and collaborations. This can help you grow your business and achieve your goals.

Ethics of Networking

In networking it is also important to maintain ethical standards and best practices. We shall also look at the best practices for networking, including how to follow up with your connections and how to maintain professionalism in your interactions.Ethics are the moral principles and values that guide the behavior of individuals and organizations. In networking, ethical principles guide how individuals should interact with others in a professional setting. These principles include honesty, integrity, respect, and confidentiality.

- **Honesty**

Honesty is an essential principle in networking that involves being truthful about your qualifications, experience, and intentions. Being honest helps to build trust between individuals, and trust is crucial for establishing lasting relationships. When networking, it's essential to be truthful about your skills and experience, as exaggerating or misrepresenting yourself can ultimately damage your reputation and hinder your ability to form meaningful connections.

For example, let's say you're attending a networking event, and someone asks about your experience in a particular field. You may be tempted to exaggerate your experience to appear more qualified than you actually are. However, if you're not truthful about your experience, the other person may eventually find out, which can lead to mistrust and damage your professional relationship.

Being honest also involves being transparent about your intentions when networking. For instance, if you're attending a networking event to seek employment opportunities, it's essential to be honest about your job search status. By being upfront about your intentions, you can build trust with potential employers and establish a positive professional relationship.

- **Integrity**

Integrity is a crucial principle in networking that involves being honest and transparent in your actions and decisions. Individuals with integrity are often trusted by others and are more likely to be successful in their careers. When networking, it's important to act with integrity, as it can help establish a positive reputation and foster trust with potential business partners or clients.

For instance, let's say you promise to introduce someone to a potential client or employer. To act with integrity, it's essential to follow through on that promise. If you fail to follow through, it can lead to disappointment and frustration for the person who was expecting your help. It can also damage your reputation as someone who doesn't keep their word, which can harm your ability to establish meaningful professional relationships.

- **Respect**

Respect is a fundamental principle in networking that involves treating others with dignity and recognizing their worth and value. When networking, it's essential to be respectful of others' time, opinions, and beliefs. By showing respect, you can build trust and establish positive professional relationships.

For example, when meeting someone for the first time, it's crucial to show respect by actively listening to what they have to say and showing genuine interest in their ideas and perspectives. By doing so, you can demonstrate that you value their opinions and are willing to learn from them.

In addition, showing respect in networking involves being mindful of others' time and schedules. For instance, if you're scheduling a meeting or phone call with someone, it's essential to be punctual and respect their time. If you need to reschedule, it's important to give them plenty of notice and offer alternative times that work for both parties.

Furthermore, showing respect in networking involves being mindful of others' beliefs and cultures. For example, if you're networking with individuals from different cultural backgrounds, it's important to be aware of cultural norms and customs. By showing respect for different cultures and beliefs, you can build trust and establish positive professional relationships.

- **Confidentiality**

Confidentiality is a critical principle in networking that involves respecting the privacy of others and safeguarding their sensitive or confidential information. When networking, individuals may share personal, financial, or business-related information that should not be disclosed to others without permission. By keeping this information confidential, you can build trust and establish positive professional relationships.

For instance, let's say you're attending a networking event, and you strike up a conversation with a potential business partner. During the conversation, they mention that they're planning to launch a new product and provide you with some details about the product and their business strategy. To act with confidentiality, it's essential to keep this information confidential and not share it with others without their permission.

Furthermore, acting with confidentiality in networking involves being mindful of how you store and share information. For example, if you receive confidential information via email, it's essential to use secure methods to store and transmit that information. You should also be aware of who has access to that information and ensure that it's not accessible to unauthorized individuals.

By respecting the confidentiality of others, you can establish trust and credibility in your professional relationships. It's important to note that breaches of confidentiality can lead to legal and reputational consequences for both individuals and organizations.

Best Practices for Networking

1. Be prepared: Before attending a networking event or meeting, it's essential to be prepared. Research the event or the person you're meeting with, and be ready to discuss topics related to their interests or industries. Being prepared shows that you're serious about building a relationship and can help you make a good first impression.

2. Be Genuine: When networking, it's important to be yourself and show genuine interest in others. Avoid being too aggressive or pushy, as this can turn people off. Instead, focus on building relationships and showing that you're interested in others and their careers.

3. Follow up: Following up is an essential part of networking. After meeting with someone, it's important to follow up with them and thank them for their time. You can also use this opportunity to continue the conversation and discuss potential opportunities or collaborations.

4. Maintain professionalism: When networking, it's essential to maintain professionalism in your interactions. This includes being punctual, dressing appropriately, and avoiding controversial topics. Maintaining professionalism shows that you're serious about building a relationship and can help you establish a positive reputation.

Networking involves building and maintaining relationships with others. Here are some best practices for networking that can help you build strong relationships with others and advance your career.

Networking is an essential skill for success in today's world. By building a strong network and leveraging it for success, you can stay ahead of the competition, expand your knowledge and skills, and create new opportunities for growth and development. Remember, the power of networking lies in the relationships you build and the value you provide to others. So, start building your network today and see where it takes you.

During the Trojan War, the Greeks demonstrated an extraordinary example of collaboration and networking as they sought to conquer the city of Troy. Recognizing the importance of unity, they formed alliances with different Greek city-states, bringing together a diverse array of leaders, warriors, and resources. Led by figures such as Agamemnon, Menelaus, Achilles, and Odysseus, the Greeks leveraged their connections and persuasive skills to foster a sense of shared purpose and commitment. This networking enabled them to pool their strengths and establish a formidable force against Troy.

Through these alliances, the Greeks not only expanded their military capabilities but also fostered a spirit of cooperation and mutual support. They exchanged valuable information, shared intelligence on Trojan defenses, and strategized collectively. This collaborative approach allowed them to adapt their tactics and exploit the weaknesses of Troy, ultimately leading to their victory.

Moreover, networking played a vital role in inspiring courage and motivation among the Greek forces. The shared bonds formed through their collaborations nurtured a sense of camaraderie and camaraderie, strengthening their resolve and determination to achieve their goal. The warriors fought side by side, supporting and relying on one another, creating a powerful network of trust and solidarity.

One of the most notable examples of their collaborative effort was the construction of the Trojan Horse. This masterful plan involved the combined skills and contributions of Greek warriors. Through effective communication and coordination, they built a massive wooden horse, concealing elite fighters within it. This ingenious strategy relied on the trust and connections established among the Greeks, as they successfully infiltrated Troy and turned the tide of the war in their favor.

The Greek networking and collaborative efforts during the Trojan War serve as a timeless testament to the power of unity and collective action. By leveraging their connections, fostering alliances, and embracing collaboration, the Greeks showcased the transformative impact of working together towards a common goal. This serves as an inspiring example for individuals today, highlighting the immense potential that can be unlocked through networking and collaboration in pursuit of personal and collective success.

The Hellenistic League, formed after the death of Alexander the Great, exemplifies the importance of networking among various kingdoms and empires for success. Networking played a pivotal role in maintaining stability, defending against external threats, and fostering cooperation among these Hellenistic states. Through diplomatic negotiations, alliances, and the establishment of personal connections, the Hellenistic rulers recognized the significance of collaboration to safeguard their territories and maintain their power.

Networking among the Hellenistic kingdoms served several purposes. Firstly, it created a sense of shared purpose and unity among the rulers. By forging alliances and maintaining communication channels, they were able to coordinate their efforts and respond effectively to external challenges. These networks facilitated the exchange of information, military strategies, and intelligence, enabling the Hellenistic rulers to stay informed and adapt to changing circumstances.

Furthermore, networking promoted mutual support and resource sharing. Through marriages, alliances, and trade agreements, the Hellenistic rulers were able to pool their resources, including military forces, financial wealth, and technological advancements. This collaborative approach allowed them to confront common enemies, such as rival empires or ambitious neighboring states, with combined strength and coordinated military campaigns.

The networking strategies employed by the Hellenistic League find a parallel in the modern-day concept of social media and other digital networking tools. Just as the Hellenistic rulers formed alliances and cultivated personal connections for mutual benefit, modern networking tools like social media provide individuals with platforms to connect, collaborate, and share ideas. Platforms such as LinkedIn, Facebook, Twitter, and Instagram allow professionals to build networks, engage with peers, and access a wealth of information and resources. Through these digital networks, individuals can expand their reach, establish connections across industries and geographies, and leverage the collective knowledge and support of their online communities. This parallel emphasizes the enduring importance of networking in both ancient and modern times as a means to achieve success, foster collaboration, and seize opportunities in an interconnected world.

ᚦᚦᚦ

Summary

In this chapter, we delved into the significance of networking and its role in building a strong foundation for success. Networking goes beyond simply accumulating contacts; it involves fostering authentic connections with like-minded individuals who share similar values and aspirations. A robust network can serve as a gateway to various opportunities, including access to knowledge, support systems, collaborative endeavors, and personal and professional growth. We learned that networking is a reciprocal process, wherein both parties contribute and reap the benefits. By carefully selecting the right individuals to connect with, investing time and effort into cultivating meaningful relationships, and offering value to others, we can construct a network that propels us towards our desired outcomes. We also explored the ethical principles that underpin networking, such as honesty, integrity, respect, and confidentiality, which guide our professional interactions. Furthermore, we examined strategies for leveraging our network to achieve success, such as gaining market insights, seeking feedback, continuous learning, and creating new opportunities. Overall, networking is an essential skill in today's competitive landscape, enabling us to stay ahead, make well-informed decisions, and realize our goals.

Activity: Enhancing Networking Skills for Success

1. *Attend Networking Events: Seek out industry-specific conferences, seminars, or social gatherings where you can meet professionals in your field of interest. Engage in conversations, exchange business cards, and follow up with individuals who resonate with your goals and aspirations.*

2. *Join Professional Associations: Identify relevant professional associations or organizations related to your field and become an active member. Attend meetings, participate in committees, and contribute to discussions to expand your network and establish yourself as a valuable resource.*

3. *Develop a Networking Elevator Pitch: Craft a concise and compelling introduction that highlights your skills, experiences, and goals. Practice delivering it confidently and adapt it based on the context and the individuals you are connecting with.*

4. *Utilize Social Media: Leverage social media platforms such as LinkedIn, Twitter, or industry-specific forums to connect with professionals and engage in relevant discussions. Share valuable insights, contribute to conversations, and build your online presence as a knowledgeable and approachable individual.*

5. *Offer Help and Support: Actively seek opportunities to provide assistance or support to your network. Offer your expertise, share relevant resources or connections, and be genuinely interested in helping others succeed. This fosters goodwill and strengthens your relationships.*

6. *Cultivate Authentic Relationships: Focus on building genuine connections rather than merely collecting contacts. Take an interest in others' journeys, listen actively, and find*

common ground. Authenticity and sincerity go a long way in establishing trust and long-lasting relationships.

7. *Follow Up and Stay Connected: After initial meetings or conversations, make it a point to follow up with individuals. Send personalized emails or messages expressing your appreciation for their time and expressing your interest in staying connected. Schedule periodic check-ins to nurture relationships over time.*

8. *Seek Mentorship: Identify professionals who have achieved success in your desired field and approach them to be your mentor. A mentor can provide guidance, support, and valuable insights as you navigate your career path.*

9. *Attend Workshops and Webinars: Stay updated with industry trends and developments by attending workshops, webinars, or online courses. These platforms not only enhance your knowledge but also provide opportunities to connect with experts and fellow participants.*

10. *Be Proactive and Take Initiative: Actively seek opportunities to initiate conversations, collaborate on projects, or propose innovative ideas within your network. Taking the initiative showcases your enthusiasm, drive, and commitment to success.*

Remember, networking is a continuous process that requires consistent effort and genuine engagement. By actively participating in these activities, you can enhance your networking skills, expand your professional connections, and create valuable opportunities for personal and career growth.

FOUR

SAILING THE INTERNET SEAS: NAVIGATING WITH WISDOM

"The internet can be an amazing tool, but it can also be a breeding ground for hate, prejudice, and disinformation. So it's up to all of us to use it wisely, to be good digital citizens, and to build communities of trust and respect online." - Michelle Obama.

ᐱᐱᐱ

Life without the internet was undoubtedly a different experience, filled with its own unique rhythms and dynamics. Back in those days, time seemed to move at a different pace. Without the constant distractions and instant connectivity of the digital world, people had more time to immerse themselves in activities, connect with others on a deeper level, and engage with the world around them.

Before the internet, daily life was not dominated by screens and notifications. People had to rely on more traditional forms of communication, such as face-to-face conversations, phone calls, or handwritten letters. These interactions required patience and effort, but they also provided a sense of genuine connection and intimacy. Conversations were unhurried, and attention was fully focused on the present moment.

In the absence of the internet's vast sea of information, people relied on books, newspapers, and magazines for knowledge and entertainment. This meant dedicating uninterrupted time to reading, allowing for deep dives into subjects of interest. There was a sense of discovery and exploration, as one had to actively seek out information rather than having it instantaneously available at their fingertips.

Without the constant influx of news, updates, and social media feeds, individuals had more control over their attention and mental space. They were not bombarded with a never-ending stream of notifications, demanding instant responses or pulling them into an endless loop of scrolling. This allowed for a greater focus on personal interests, hobbies, and self-reflection.

However, it's important to note that life without the internet also had its challenges. Information was not as readily accessible, and staying updated on current events required more effort. Communication with distant friends and relatives was often slower and less frequent. Tasks that now take seconds to complete, such as online shopping or booking travel arrangements, required more time and effort.

In today's digitally connected world, time seems to pass at an accelerated pace. The constant stream of information, entertainment, and communication can create a sense of urgency and a feeling of always being "on." There is an inherent pressure to keep up with the latest trends, news, and social media updates.

However, wise internet usage allows us to strike a balance. It means being intentional and mindful about how we engage with the online world. It's about setting boundaries, carving out designated periods of uninterrupted time, and consciously choosing how we spend our digital moments. By doing so, we can reclaim a sense of control over our time, ensuring that we use the internet as a tool to enhance our lives rather than letting it consume us.

In this chapter, we will explore the impact of the internet on our perception of time and how we can navigate the digital landscape with wisdom. We will delve into strategies for mindful internet usage, time management, and striking a healthy balance between online and offline experiences. By finding harmony in our digital lives, we can create space for deeper connections, personal growth, and a greater sense of fulfillment in the fast-paced world we inhabit.

Let's take a moment to reflect on how we use the internet. How often do we find ourselves mindlessly scrolling through social media feeds or getting lost in the endless abyss of cat videos and memes? While the internet offers a wealth of information and opportunities, it can also be a significant source of distraction and time-wasting. So, how can we utilize the internet wisely to maximize our success and avoid falling into unproductive habits?

Imagine the internet as a vast library, filled with knowledge and resources at our fingertips. Just as in a physical library, we must approach it with intention and purpose. Instead of aimlessly browsing, we can make a conscious effort to seek out valuable information, educational resources, and opportunities for growth. Whether it's learning a new skill, gaining industry insights, or expanding our knowledge, the internet provides a wealth of platforms and resources to help us on our journey to success.

Let's consider the power of online learning. With access to countless online courses, webinars, and tutorials, we can develop new skills or enhance existing ones from the comfort of our own homes. Whether it's mastering a programming language, improving our public speaking abilities, or honing our leadership skills, the internet offers a multitude of platforms, such as Coursera, Udemy, and LinkedIn Learning, to help us acquire knowledge and grow professionally. By utilizing these resources effectively, we can take proactive steps towards achieving our goals and advancing our careers.

In addition to formal educational opportunities, the internet also provides access to a vast network of experts and thought leaders. Online communities, forums, and social media platforms offer opportunities to connect with individuals who share our interests and passions. Engaging in meaningful conversations and exchanging ideas with like-minded individuals not only expands our knowledge but also opens doors to potential collaborations and mentorship. By harnessing the power of online networks, we can build valuable relationships that contribute to our personal and professional success.

However, it is important to be discerning consumers of information. With the internet's vastness comes the challenge of distinguishing between reliable sources and misinformation. In a world of clickbait headlines and sensationalism, it is crucial to develop critical thinking skills and verify the credibility of the information we come across. By fact-checking, cross-referencing multiple sources, and seeking out reputable platforms, we can ensure that we are accessing accurate and trustworthy information that adds value to our lives and endeavors.

Let's not forget the importance of maintaining a healthy balance in our internet usage. While the internet can be a powerful tool for success, it is essential to set boundaries and avoid falling into the trap of excessive screen time and mindless scrolling. Being mindful of how we allocate our time online can help us prioritize tasks, manage our productivity, and prevent the internet from becoming a source of distraction. Setting specific time limits, creating a schedule, and practicing self-discipline are effective strategies to ensure that we are utilizing the internet in a way that aligns with our goals and aspirations.

Now, let's take a moment to reflect on our own internet usage. Are there any areas where we can make improvements? How can we incorporate the principles of intentionality, discernment, and balance into our online activities? By consciously using the internet as a tool for growth and success, we can navigate the vast digital landscape with purpose and achieve meaningful results.

Remember, the internet is a powerful resource that, when used wisely, can propel us towards success. By leveraging online learning, connecting with experts and communities, and practicing discernment and balance, we can harness the full potential of the internet to support our personal and professional aspirations. So, let's approach the internet with intention and embrace the opportunities it offers, making the most of this remarkable tool on our journey to success.

Maintaining a healthy balance in our internet usage is paramount. The internet has a way of capturing our attention and leading us down rabbit holes of distraction. Setting clear boundaries and being mindful of our online activities can help us maximize productivity and prevent the internet from becoming a time sink. Practicing time management techniques, such as the Pomodoro Technique or setting specific time blocks for online activities, can help us stay focused and accomplish our goals. It's also important to allocate time for offline activities, such as exercise, hobbies, and face-to-face interactions, which contribute to overall well-being and personal growth.

In addition to using the internet as a tool for personal success, it can also be leveraged for entrepreneurial endeavors. The internet provides a platform for launching businesses, reaching a global audience, and creating an online presence. Through e-commerce, social media marketing, and digital advertising, individuals can establish and grow their own ventures. The internet enables access to a vast customer base, facilitates efficient communication and collaboration, and offers innovative solutions to various business challenges. By harnessing the power of the internet, entrepreneurs can amplify their reach, scale their operations, and achieve remarkable success.

Ultimately, using the internet wisely for success requires intention, discipline, and a focus on quality over quantity. By identifying our goals, leveraging online resources strategically, and exercising discernment, we can optimize our internet usage for maximum impact. Embracing the potential of online learning, networking, critical thinking, and balanced usage empowers us to navigate the digital landscape with purpose and achieve our aspirations.

So, as you reflect on your own internet usage, consider how you can harness its potential to propel yourself towards success. How can you incorporate online learning into your personal and professional development? Which communities and thought leaders can you connect with to expand your network and gain valuable insights? How will you ensure the accuracy and credibility of the information you consume? And, most importantly, how will you strike a healthy balance between online and offline activities to maximize productivity and well-being?

By consciously utilizing the internet as a powerful tool, you can unlock a world of possibilities, broaden your horizons, and accelerate your journey towards success. Embrace the opportunities it offers, while maintaining a mindful approach, and watch as it becomes a catalyst for personal and professional growth. The internet is a remarkable resource—it's up to you to make the most of it on your

In this chapter, we will explore the importance of using the Internet wisely, and offer some tips on how to avoid getting addicted to it.

The Benefits of Using the Internet Wisely:

1. Access to Information: The Internet provides us with access to a vast amount of information, which we can use to expand our knowledge and improve our skills. We can learn about almost anything, from history and

science to art and literature.

2. Communication: The Internet has made communication easier than ever before. We can communicate with people all over the world instantly, and for free. This has opened up opportunities for collaboration, networking, and making new friends.

3. Entertainment: The Internet provides us with endless sources of entertainment, from streaming movies and TV shows to playing online games. It can be a great way to unwind and relax after a long day.

Using the internet wisely is crucial for professionals as it can greatly impact their careers and personal lives, it's also important to recognize that the internet can be a double-edged sword, and its overuse or misuse can have negative consequences.

One of the primary reasons why using the internet wisely is essential for professionals is that it can affect their mental health and well-being. Spending excessive amounts of time on the internet can lead to feelings of isolation, anxiety, and depression. It can also contribute to a lack of focus, decreased productivity, and burnout, which can ultimately impact one's career and job performance.

Moreover, not having control over one's internet usage can lead to addiction, which is characterized by compulsive and excessive use of the internet despite negative consequences. Internet addiction can have detrimental effects on a person's physical, emotional, and social well-being and can lead to negative consequences such as reduced work performance, strained relationships, and financial problems.

In addition to the negative effects on mental health and well-being, uncontrolled internet usage can also have a detrimental impact on one's career. For instance, posting inappropriate content on social media can damage one's professional reputation and hinder career advancement opportunities. Similarly, using the internet to engage in unethical or illegal activities can lead to legal and reputational consequences that can have long-lasting effects on one's career and personal life.

Therefore, using the internet wisely is crucial for professionals to maintain their mental health, well-being, and career success. By setting boundaries, practicing self-discipline, and using the internet for professional and personal growth in a responsible manner, professionals can reap the benefits of the internet while minimizing its negative effects.

According to a survey conducted by the Pew Research Center in 2021, 91% of adults in the United States use the internet, with 31% reporting that they go online "almost constantly." Additionally, studies have shown that internet addiction is prevalent in many other countries, including China, South Korea, and Japan.

Internet addiction has been linked to a range of negative effects on mental and physical health. In a study published in the Journal of Behavioral Addictions, researchers found that internet addiction was associated with symptoms of depression, anxiety, and poor sleep quality. Another study published in the International Journal of Mental Health and Addiction found that internet addiction was associated with decreased academic performance and lower levels of social support.

The harmful effects of internet addiction are particularly pronounced in children and teenagers. According to a report by the World Health Organization, excessive screen time in children can lead to a range of health problems, including obesity, poor sleep, and impaired cognitive development. Additionally, studies have shown that internet addiction can lead to social isolation, decreased social skills, and a higher risk of mental health problems.

To address the problem of internet addiction, many countries have implemented policies and programs aimed at promoting healthy internet use. For example, in South Korea, internet addiction is recognized as a public health crisis, and the government has implemented a range of programs aimed at preventing and treating the condition. Similarly, in China, the government has launched a nationwide campaign to combat internet addiction, including the establishment of treatment centers and the implementation of regulations on online gaming.

Despite these efforts, internet addiction continues to be a significant problem globally. As technology continues to advance and become more integrated into our daily lives, it is essential that we take steps to promote healthy internet use and address the harmful effects of internet addiction. This may include developing public awareness campaigns, implementing policies and regulations to limit screen time and promote healthy habits, and investing in research aimed at understanding and addressing the root causes of internet addiction.

There are numberous stories of internet addiction, one real-life story of a person who struggled with internet addiction is the case of Ryan Van Cleave. Ryan was a college professor and writer who became addicted to online gaming and social media. He spent hours each day playing games and scrolling through social media feeds, neglecting his responsibilities and relationships.

Ryan's addiction began to take a toll on his personal and professional life. He missed deadlines for his writing projects, neglected his teaching duties, and became distant from his family and friends. He also developed physical health problems, including headaches and eye strain, from spending so much time in front of a screen.

Eventually, Ryan hit rock bottom when he was fired from his job as a college professor due to his addiction. He realized that he needed help and sought treatment for his addiction. He started attending support groups and therapy sessions to learn how to manage his internet use and regain control of his life.

Today, Ryan has overcome his addiction and is back on track with his writing career. He has written a memoir about his experience, titled "Unplugged: My Journey into the Dark World of Video Game Addiction," to raise awareness about the dangers of internet addiction and encourage others to seek help if they are struggling with similar issues.

Ryan's story serves as a cautionary tale about the dangers of internet addiction and the importance of using the internet responsibly. It is essential to maintain a healthy balance between online and offline activities to avoid the negative consequences of internet addiction.

One real-life story of internet addiction leading to a ruined life is the case of Xu Yuyuan, a Chinese teenager who became addicted to online gaming.

Xu Yuyuan started playing online games when he was 14 years old and quickly became obsessed with them. He would spend hours each day playing games and neglecting his studies and social life. His parents tried to intervene and limit his internet use, but he became increasingly defiant and started skipping school to play games.

Eventually, Xu dropped out of school and became a full-time online gamer. He would spend all of his time playing games and neglecting his personal hygiene and health. He developed a serious addiction to gaming and began experiencing withdrawal symptoms when he was away from his computer.

Xu's addiction eventually led to a tragic ending. In 2007, at the age of 17, he died of exhaustion and dehydration after playing online games for several days straight. His parents found him collapsed in his chair in front of his computer, and he was pronounced dead at the hospital.

Xu's story is a tragic example of how internet addiction can lead to a ruined life. It is a stark reminder of the importance of using the internet responsibly and maintaining a healthy balance between online and offline activities.

ᐁᐁᐁ

Brian and Harvey had been colleagues for some time now though they had been in different department after their individual promotions. Being friends from childhood they cared about each other. Harvey like Brian was an incredibly talented developer, but he had developed a problem off late and was not vocal about it: he was addicted to the internet.

At first, it was just a few hours a day, but gradually, it became an obsession. Harvey would spend hours on social media, watching videos, and online shopping, ignoring his work and responsibilities. His addiction became so bad that he would even skip meals and forget to sleep. Brian was concerned about Harvey's behavior, but he didn't know how to approach him. It was only when Harvey's work started suffering, and he was on the verge of losing his job that Brian decided to step in. One day, Brian invited Harvey over to his house and had an honest conversation with him. He shared his own struggles with internet addiction and told Harvey how he overcame it. He advised Harvey to set clear goals and priorities for his work and personal life, and to schedule specific times for checking emails and social media. He also suggested taking breaks and doing physical activities to keep the mind fresh. Initially, Harvey was resistant and didn't believe that he had a problem. But as he followed Brian's advice, he started to see a difference. He became more productive at work, and his personal life improved. He realized that he had been wasting valuable time on the internet and that he had to be more mindful of how he used it. Over time, Harvey's addiction subsided, and he became more focused on his work and personal goals. He was grateful to Brian for his intervention and support, and they became closer than ever. The experience taught Harvey the importance of time management and being mindful of how he used the internet. He promised to continue implementing Brian's tips and to help others who might be struggling with internet addiction. As for Brian, he felt fulfilled knowing that he was able to help his friend and prevent him from losing his job. He continued to work on innovative solutions and remained mindful of his internet use. The two friends remained close and were an inspiration to others in their company.

ppp

Internet addiction is a growing problem affecting people of all ages. With the increasing prevalence of smartphones, social media, and online entertainment, it's easy to get hooked on the internet and spend hours mindlessly scrolling through content. This addiction can have a significant impact on our mental and physical health, as well as our relationships and careers.

To overcome internet addiction, it's essential to recognize the signs of addiction and take steps to break the cycle. One common symptom of internet addiction is spending more time online than intended and neglecting other responsibilities such as work, school, or social relationships. Another symptom is feeling anxious or irritable when away from the internet or when internet access is limited.

To use the internet wisely, it's important to set boundaries and establish limits on our internet usage. This may include limiting the amount of time spent online, creating a schedule for internet use, or setting specific goals for internet use. Additionally, it's important to engage in activities that promote well-being, such as exercise, socializing, or pursuing hobbies or interests offline.

Mindfulness practices such as meditation or journaling can also be helpful in overcoming internet addiction. These practices can help us become more aware of our thoughts and behaviors and develop greater control over our impulses. By becoming more mindful, we can learn to identify triggers for internet use and develop strategies for managing them.

Ultimately, overcoming internet addiction requires a willingness to change and a commitment to self-care. It may also involve seeking professional help or joining support groups to connect with others who are struggling with internet addiction. With effort and perseverance, it's possible to break free from the cycle of internet addiction and use the internet in a way that supports our well-being and personal growth.

Avoiding Internet Addiction:

1. Set Limits: Set a limit on the amount of time you spend on the Internet each day. This will help you avoid spending too much time online and getting addicted.
2. Take Breaks: Take regular breaks from the Internet, especially if you have been using it for a long time. This will help you stay focused and avoid getting distracted.
3. Prioritize Real-Life Interactions: Remember to prioritize real-life interactions over online interactions. Make time to spend with friends and family in person, and engage in hobbies and activities that don't involve the Internet.
4. Use Technology to Help You: There are many apps and tools available that can help you manage your Internet usage. For example, you can use a timer app to limit the amount of time you spend on social media each day.

In conclusion, the Internet can be a valuable tool, but it is important to use it wisely and avoid getting addicted to it. By setting limits, taking breaks, prioritizing real-life interactions, and using technology to help you, you can ensure that the Internet is a positive force in your life.

ᗇᗇᗇ

Chapter Summary

This chapter explored the growing problem of internet addiction and its significant impact on various aspects of our lives. It emphasized the importance of recognizing the signs of internet addiction and taking proactive steps to break the cycle. The summary highlighted key strategies for overcoming internet addiction, including setting clear goals and priorities, scheduling specific times for online activities, and incorporating offline activities into our daily routine. The chapter emphasized the importance of building healthy habits, practicing self-discipline, and seeking support from friends, family, or professionals. By being mindful of our internet usage and using it as a tool for personal and professional growth, we were able to overcome internet addiction and regain control over our lives.

Activity

Here are some suggested activities to help us avoid becoming addicted to the internet:

1. *Pursue hobbies and interests: Explore activities like painting, playing a musical instrument, gardening, or cooking. Engaging in offline hobbies helps to diversify your interests and provides a break from excessive internet use.*
2. *Read books: Immerse yourself in the world of literature. Reading not only enhances knowledge but also stimulates imagination and creativity.*
3. *Spend time with family and friends: Foster meaningful relationships by spending quality time with loved ones. Engage in conversations, play games, or plan outings together.*
4. *Outdoor activities: Enjoy the beauty of nature by going for walks, hiking, cycling, or participating in sports. It promotes physical well-being and reduces dependence on the internet.*
5. *Volunteer or engage in community service: Contribute positively to society by volunteering at local organizations, participating in charity events, or helping those in need. It provides a sense of fulfillment and builds a strong sense of community.*

6. *Learn new skills: Explore offline learning opportunities like attending workshops, joining classes or clubs, or pursuing a new hobby. Acquiring new skills enhances personal growth and expands horizons.*
7. *Practice mindfulness and self-reflection: Engage in activities like meditation, journaling, or practicing yoga to improve mental well-being, self-awareness, and reduce reliance on constant online stimulation.*

Remember, striking a balance between online and offline activities is crucial for a healthy and fulfilling life.

FIVE

BEYOND COMPARISON: DISCOVERING TRUE HAPPINESS WITHIN YOURSELF

"Comparison is the thief of joy." - Theodore Roosevelt

ᐅᐅᐅ

"No Comparison: The Key to Happiness" is a powerful concept that can help us live a more fulfilling and satisfying life. When we stop comparing ourselves to others, we can focus on our own strengths, values, and goals. Here are some examples of how "No Comparison" can lead to greater happiness:

The habit of comparing ourselves with others is deeply ingrained in our society, and it starts from a very early age. We are often compared with our siblings, classmates, and friends, and this comparison continues throughout our lives. While healthy competition can motivate us to achieve our goals, constantly comparing ourselves with others can lead to misery and unhappiness.

Scientific research has shown that people who constantly compare themselves with others are more likely to experience negative emotions such as envy, jealousy, and anxiety. One study found that social comparison can lead to decreased well-being and increased levels of stress, especially if the comparison is made with someone who is perceived to be more successful or better off.

Furthermore, comparison with others can lead to a distorted view of reality, as people tend to only compare themselves with those who are doing better than them, and not with those who are worse off. This can create a never-ending cycle of dissatisfaction and feelings of inadequacy.

To break free from the habit of comparing ourselves with others, we need to focus on our own progress and growth, and not on the achievements of others. We should also learn to appreciate what we have and be grateful for our blessings. By doing so, we can cultivate a positive and healthy mindset, which will lead to greater happiness and fulfillment in life.

There are several causes of comparison with others in life. One of the primary reasons is our need for social acceptance and belonging. We tend to compare ourselves with others to gauge where we stand in society and to assess our worth in comparison to others. This need for social validation can stem from our upbringing, cultural values, and societal norms.

Another reason for comparison is the desire for success and achievement. We often compare ourselves with others who we perceive to be more successful in their careers, relationships, or financial status. This can create a sense of pressure to achieve similar success, which can be motivating but can also lead to feelings of inadequacy and unhappiness.

The media and advertising also play a significant role in fueling the habit of comparison with others. We are constantly bombarded with images of the "perfect" body, lifestyle, and possessions, which can create unrealistic expectations and lead to a distorted view of reality.

Moreover, personality traits such as perfectionism, low self-esteem, and a need for control can also contribute to the tendency to compare ourselves with others. These traits can create a sense of insecurity and self-doubt, leading us to seek validation through comparison with others.

In summary, the causes of comparison with others are multifaceted and can stem from social, cultural, psychological, and media-related factors. It is important to identify and understand these causes to develop a healthy and positive mindset, free from the pitfalls of constant comparison with others.

There are several modern trends that can push us into the pitfall of comparison in our day-to-day lives, including:

1. Social Media: Social media platforms are often a breeding ground for comparison. We see others 'highlight reels and compare our own lives to theirs, which can lead to feelings of inadequacy and low self-esteem. By focusing on our own journey and progress, we can find greater joy and satisfaction in our own lives.

2. Material Possessions: It is easy to fall into the trap of comparing our material possessions to others. We may feel that we need the latest gadgets, clothes, or cars to keep up with those around us. However, when we realize that these things do not bring lasting happiness, we can focus on cultivating meaningful relationships, experiences, and personal growth.

3. Career Success: Many of us feel pressure to achieve certain levels of success in our careers. We compare our progress to that of our colleagues and peers, which can lead to feelings of stress and burnout. When we focus on our own goals and values, we can find greater satisfaction in our work and avoid the negative effects of comparison.

4. Physical Appearance: The media bombards us with images of "ideal" beauty, which can lead to feelings of insecurity and low self-esteem. By focusing on our own unique qualities and strengths, we can find greater confidence and self-acceptance.

5. Advertisements: The advertising industry has become a major force in shaping our society, and it plays a significant role in promoting comparison among individuals. Advertisements constantly bombard us with messages that suggest we need certain products to look and feel better, to be more successful, or to fit in with the crowd. These messages can create a sense of inadequacy and pressure to keep up with the latest trends and fashions. We are constantly bombarded with images of beautiful people with perfect bodies, designer clothes, and luxury cars, and this can create a strong desire to achieve the same level of success and status.

"Keeping up with the Joneses" is a cultural phenomenon that has been around for a long time. It refers to the desire to match or exceed the social status or possessions of our neighbors. This trend can create a sense of pressure to compete with others, and it can lead to overspending, debt, and financial stress. The pressure to keep up with the Joneses can be especially challenging in our social media-driven society, where people are constantly sharing and showcasing their accomplishments and possessions. This can make it challenging for people to feel content and satisfied with what they have. To stay away from the trap of "keeping up with the Joneses," it is essential to recognize that material possessions do not necessarily equate to happiness. People should focus on their values and prioritize their spending based on their needs and not what they think they should have. It is also essential to create a budget and stick to it, avoiding unnecessary spending on items that won't add value to our lives.

Overall, "No Comparison" is a powerful concept that can help us find greater happiness and fulfillment in our lives. When we focus on our own journey and progress, we can live more authentically and find joy in our own unique experiences.

Consumerism is a culture of buying and consuming goods and services, often to keep up with trends or match our peers' lifestyles. Constantly comparing ourselves with others' possessions and consumer choices can lead to a sense of inadequacy and pressure to keep up. This can result in overspending, debt, and financial stress. To stay away from this trap, it is crucial to develop a conscious and mindful approach to consumption. It is essential to understand our needs versus wants and prioritize our spending accordingly. We can practice mindful consumption by focusing on quality rather than quantity, buying products that are durable and environmentally friendly, and avoiding impulse buying. Additionally, we can practice gratitude and appreciate what we already have rather than constantly striving for more. We can also try to cultivate hobbies or activities that do not involve spending money, such as spending time in nature, reading, or spending time with loved ones. By developing a conscious and mindful approach to consumption, we can break free from the trap of consumerism and live a more fulfilling and sustainable life.

Throughout history, there have been numerous examples of how comparison with others can have negative impacts on individuals and society as a whole. One of the most well-known examples is the French Revolution. The French monarchy and aristocracy lived extravagant lifestyles, with lavish parties, luxurious homes, and expensive clothing, while the majority of the population struggled to make ends meet. This stark contrast between the rich and poor fueled resentment and led to the revolution, which ended in violence and upheaval.

Another example is the rise of the Nazi party in Germany in the early 20th century. The Nazi party promoted the idea of Aryan superiority, leading to the persecution and murder of millions of people deemed inferior, including Jews, homosexuals, and people with disabilities. This ideology was fueled by a sense of comparison and competition with other nations and races, leading to devastating consequences.

In modern times, social media has led to a surge in comparison culture, leading to negative impacts on mental health and well-being. People often present a curated and filtered version of their lives on social media, leading others to feel inadequate or inferior. This can result in a sense of pressure to live up to unrealistic standards and can lead to feelings of anxiety and depression.

These examples from history demonstrate how comparison with others can have negative impacts on individuals and society as a whole. It is essential to understand that everyone has a unique journey and that comparing ourselves to others is not a sustainable or healthy approach to life. Instead, we should focus on our own goals, values, and priorities and strive to live a fulfilling and meaningful life that aligns with our own needs and aspirations.

Achilles and Hector were two legendary warriors from Greek mythology, who are often remembered for their fierce rivalry and tragic fates. The story of their comparison is a cautionary tale about the dangers of pride and ego, and the destructive consequences of envy and jealousy.

Achilles was the son of a sea goddess and a mortal king, and was known for his exceptional strength and courage. He was considered by many to be the greatest warrior of his time, and his reputation for invincibility on the battlefield was widely known.

Hector, on the other hand, was the prince of Troy, and was known for his bravery, honor, and devotion to his city and people. He was a skilled warrior and leader, and was highly respected by his fellow Trojans.

Despite their differences, Achilles and Hector were both consumed by their own pride and ego, and were constantly comparing themselves to each other. Achilles was jealous of Hector's honor and reputation, while Hector was envious of Achilles' strength and invincibility.

Their rivalry came to a head during the Trojan War, when Hector killed Achilles' best friend Patroclus in battle.

This act of aggression fueled Achilles' rage and led him to seek revenge against Hector.

In the end, Achilles and Hector faced each other in a one-on-one battle, which ultimately resulted in Hector's death. Achilles was consumed by his own pride and ego, and desecrated Hector's body, dragging it around the city of Troy in triumph.

However, Achilles' victory was short-lived, as he was killed soon after by an arrow to the heel, which was his only vulnerable spot. This tragic ending serves as a powerful reminder of the dangers of comparison, pride, and ego, and the destructive consequences of envy and jealousy.

Karna and Arjuna were two of the greatest warriors from the epic Mahabharata, and their rivalry and constant battle serve as a cautionary tale about the dangers of comparison and pride, and the importance of staying true to oneself.

Karna was the eldest son of Kunti, born before her marriage to King Pandu. He was raised by a low-caste family, but became a skilled warrior and archer, earning the favor of Duryodhana, the eldest of the Kuru princes. Karna was known for his loyalty and honor, but was constantly overshadowed by Arjuna, his rival and brother raised as prince.

Arjuna, on the other hand, was the third of the Pandava brothers, and was considered by many to be the greatest warrior of his time. He was a skilled archer and strategist, and was loved by all who knew him.

Despite their differences, Karna and Arjuna were constantly compared to each other, and their rivalry became a source of constant tension and conflict. Karna was envious of Arjuna's skills and reputation, while Arjuna was jealous of Karna's natural talents and abilities.

Their rivalry came to a head during the Kurukshetra War, when Karna fought on the side of the Kauravas, while Arjuna fought on the side of the Pandavas. Karna was fiercely loyal to Duryodhana, and even when he learned the truth about his birth and his relationship to the Pandavas and Arjuna, he refused to switch sides.

Despite his bravery and skill, Karna's pride and desire for glory ultimately led to his downfall. He was cursed by his own guru, who revealed his true identity to him, and he was killed by his own brother Arjuna in a one-on-one battle.

Arjuna, on the other hand, remained true to himself and his values throughout the war, and emerged as a hero and a leader. His victory over Karna was bittersweet, as he recognized the tragic nature of their rivalry and the destructive consequences of comparison and pride.

The story of Karna and Arjuna serves as a reminder of the importance of staying true to oneself, and the dangers of comparison, envy, and pride. It is a cautionary tale that warns us against the pitfalls of ego and the destructive consequences of constantly comparing ourselves to others.

The Dangers of Comparison:

1. Comparing ourselves to others can lead to a wide range of negative emotions and behaviors, including:
2. Inadequacy: When we constantly compare ourselves to others, we may feel that we are not good enough or do not measure up to their achievements.
3. Envy: Seeing others achieve success or have things we desire can lead to feelings of envy and jealousy.
4. Low self-esteem: Comparison can lead to negative self-talk and a poor self-image, leading to lower self-esteem.

5. Unhappiness: Constant comparison can cause us to focus on what we lack rather than what we have, leading to feelings of unhappiness and discontent.

ᵱᵱᵱ

Brian and Harvey were once the best of colleagues, working together towards shared goals and mutual success. They were both accomplished in their careers, but their relationship began to sour as they fell into the trap of constantly comparing themselves to each other.

One day, Harvey arrived at the office driving a brand new sports car. Brian, who had been saving for months to buy a new car, couldn't help but feel envious. He began to resent Harvey's success and feel inferior.

Determined to keep up with Harvey, Brian impulsively purchased an expensive new car he couldn't afford. He went into debt and began to struggle to pay his bills. Harvey, meanwhile, had also been overspending to maintain his lavish lifestyle, racking up credit card debt and neglecting his savings.

As their financial situation deteriorated, their relationship became increasingly toxic. They sniped at each other in meetings, stole each other's clients, and spread rumors about one another. Their once-close friendship had turned into a bitter rivalry.

But one day, a chance encounter with a financial advisor changed everything. The advisor pointed out the flaws in their spending habits and explained how their constant comparison was hurting both their finances and their relationship.

Brian and Harvey realized that they needed to make a change. They enrolled in therapy to work through their issues and learn healthier ways to manage their emotions and finances.

Through therapy, they were able to rebuild their relationship and get back on track financially. They learned to appreciate each other's strengths and differences, rather than constantly comparing themselves to each other.

In the end, their rivalry had been a wake-up call. They emerged from therapy stronger and more resilient, with a renewed appreciation for the power of collaboration and a deep sense of gratitude for each other's friendship.

Through this shift in mindset, Brian and Harvey were able to rebuild their relationship and achieve even greater success. They began to appreciate each other's unique strengths and contributions, collaborating more effectively and achieving shared goals with greater ease.

Their story serves as a powerful reminder of the dangers of comparison and the importance of focusing on our own accomplishments and strengths. By doing so, we can not only improve our own well-being but also build stronger, more fulfilling relationships with others.

ᛈᛈᛈ

TATA is a well-known Indian conglomerate that has been successful for over 150 years. One of the key factors that have contributed to its success is its focus on values rather than cut-throat competition.

TATA has always been committed to making a positive difference in society, and this commitment is reflected in its business practices. For example, TATA Group founder Jamsetji Tata once said, "In a free enterprise, the community is not just another stakeholder in business, but in fact, the very purpose of its existence." This philosophy has guided the TATA Group's business decisions, leading to a focus on social responsibility and sustainability.

Another example of TATA's values-based approach is the company's decision to enter the automobile industry. When TATA introduced the Nano, the world's cheapest car, it was not to compete with other car manufacturers but to provide an affordable mode of transportation to millions of people in India. The Nano was a moderate success in terms of sales but received global recognition for its innovative design and TATA's efforts in making car affordable to one and all.

TATA has also been successful in the hospitality industry with its chain of luxury hotels, the Taj Group. The Taj Group is known for its exceptional service, attention to detail, and commitment to sustainability. The company's values-based approach has helped it establish a loyal customer base and win several awards for excellence in hospitality.

Overall, TATA's success can be attributed to its values-based approach, which has helped the company build a strong brand and establish a reputation for excellence. Rather than getting into cut-throat competition with other companies, TATA has always focused on making a positive difference in society, and this approach has paid off in terms of business success and customer loyalty.

Here are some effective ways to stop comparison and focus on our own unique journey:

1. Practice Gratitude: By focusing on what we have rather than what we lack, we can cultivate a sense of contentment and appreciation for our own journey. Take time each day to reflect on the things you are grateful for in your life.

2. Celebrate Your Own Accomplishments: Instead of comparing ourselves to others, celebrate our own accomplishments, no matter how small. Take time to

acknowledge your own successes and growth.

3. Reframe Negative Thoughts: When we find ourselves comparing ourselves to others, it can be helpful to reframe negative thoughts. Instead of focusing on what we lack, focus on the progress we have made and the unique qualities that make us who we are.

4. Set Goals That Align with Your Values: When we set goals that align with our own values and aspirations, we can find greater motivation and fulfillment in our journey. Take time to reflect on what truly matters to you and set goals that reflect those values.

5. Connect with Others: Surround yourself with supportive individuals who encourage and celebrate your own unique journey. Connect with those who share similar values and goals, and avoid those who perpetuate feelings of inadequacy or negativity.

Overall, the key to avoiding the trap of comparison is to focus on our own unique journey, celebrating our own successes, and cultivating gratitude and appreciation for the opportunities and experiences that come our way. By doing so, we can find greater happiness and fulfillment in our own lives.

Comparing ourselves to others is a natural human tendency, but it can lead to negative emotions and behaviors that hinder our own happiness and well-being. By recognizing that we are all on our own unique journey, we can avoid the trap of comparison and find greater fulfillment and happiness in our own lives. Cultivating gratitude, celebrating our own accomplishments, reframing negative thoughts, setting goals that align with our values, and connecting with supportive individuals are all effective strategies for avoiding the trap of comparison and finding happiness in our own journey.

When we compare ourselves with our past self, we can gain valuable insights into our growth and progress. We can analyze where we stand in terms of our learning, finances, career, personal goals, and overall clarity of thoughts. By setting realistic goals and tracking our progress, we can create a roadmap for our future success.

For example, let's say you want to improve your financial situation. By comparing your current financial status with that of last year, you can identify areas where you have improved and areas where you still need to work on. You can then set a realistic goal for the next year and track your progress towards achieving it. This approach not only helps you to stay motivated but also gives you a clear direction to work towards.

Similarly, comparison with oneself can also help in personal growth and development. If you analyze where you stand in terms of your mental and emotional well-being, you can identify patterns of behavior that may be hindering your progress. By addressing these patterns, you can develop healthier habits and achieve a more balanced and fulfilling life.

Comparing our current selves with our past selves can be a powerful tool for personal growth and success. Here are some steps to take when evaluating your progress over the past year:

1. Set goals: To effectively compare your current self with your past self, you need to have a clear idea of what you want to achieve. Set goals for yourself in areas such as career, personal development, relationships, and health.
2. Record your progress: Keep a record of your progress throughout the year. This could include journal entries,

financial statements, or work performance evaluations. Having this information will allow you to make an accurate comparison of your current self with your past self.

3. Evaluate your progress: Take time to reflect on your progress over the past year. What have you accomplished? What could you have done better? What did you learn? Consider areas where you need improvement and celebrate your successes.

4. Create an action plan: Based on your evaluation, create an action plan for the coming year. Set new goals and make a plan to achieve them. Consider what steps you can take to improve in areas where you fell short.

5. Focus on the future: Use the comparison with your past self as motivation to continue growing and improving. Look forward to the future and what you can achieve, rather than dwelling on the past.

By comparing ourselves with our past selves, we can create a roadmap for our future success. This approach allows us to focus on our own journey and personal growth rather than getting caught up in comparing ourselves with others. Remember to be kind and patient with yourself as you evaluate your progress, and use your insights to create a plan for continued success.

ppp

Chapter Summary:

In this chapter, we explored the concept of "No Comparison: The Key to Happiness" and its significance in leading a more fulfilling life. We learned that constantly comparing ourselves to others often resulted in negative emotions, such as envy, jealousy, and anxiety. These comparisons distorted our perception of reality, leading to a cycle of dissatisfaction and feelings of inadequacy.

By shifting our focus to our own progress, growth, and appreciating what we have, we discovered that we could cultivate a positive mindset and find greater happiness and fulfillment. We recognized that comparison stemmed from our need for social acceptance, the desire for success, media influence, and certain personality traits like perfectionism and low self-esteem.

Throughout history, we observed the dangers of comparison, evident in events like the French Revolution and the rise of the Nazi party. We also encountered cautionary tales from Greek mythology, with figures like Achilles and Hector, as well as characters from the Mahabharata, such as Karna and Arjuna, highlighting the destructive consequences of comparison, pride, and envy.

As we concluded this chapter, we acknowledged the detrimental impact of modern trends like social media, material possessions, career success, physical appearance, and advertising, which further fuel the habit of comparison. By embracing the principle of "No Comparison," we set ourselves on a path towards contentment, self-acceptance, and genuine happiness.

Activity:

1. *Comparisons can be a detrimental habit that hinders our happiness and self-esteem. To break free from the comparison mindset, try the following activity that encourages self-awareness and cultivates a positive outlook:*

2. *Mindful Self-Reflection: Set aside dedicated time for self-reflection without distractions. Explore the reasons behind your tendency to compare yourself to others. Is it driven by societal pressure, fear of failure, or a lack of self-confidence? Write down your thoughts and emotions, allowing yourself to gain deeper insights into your comparison patterns.*

3. *Gratitude Practice: Create a gratitude journal or use a gratitude app to regularly jot down things you appreciate about yourself and your life. Focus on your unique qualities, achievements, and experiences. Embrace gratitude for your own journey rather than comparing it to others'. Challenge yourself to find something new to be grateful for each day.*

4. *Shift Perspective: Whenever you catch yourself making comparisons, consciously shift your perspective. Remind yourself that everyone has their own unique path, and success or happiness cannot be measured solely by external factors. Train your mind to appreciate and celebrate the accomplishments of others without diminishing your own worth.*

5. *Embrace Uniqueness: Take time to identify and celebrate your own strengths, talents, and passions. Engage in activities that align with your interests and values, allowing yourself to thrive in your own unique way. Instead of striving to be like someone else, focus on becoming the best version of yourself.*

6. *Surround Yourself with Positivity: Seek out positive influences in your life. Surround yourself with supportive and encouraging people who inspire you to be your authentic self. Engage in uplifting content such as books, podcasts, or online communities that promote self-acceptance and personal growth.*

7. *Practice Self-Compassion: Treat yourself with kindness and compassion. Instead of being self-critical, acknowledge your*

strengths and weaknesses with understanding. Practice self-care and prioritize your well-being. Remember that you deserve love and acceptance, just as much as anyone else.

By engaging in these activities consistently, you can gradually shift your mindset away from comparison and embrace a more self-affirming and contented outlook. Remember, your journey is unique and incomparable, and by focusing on your own growth and happiness, you'll discover greater fulfillment in life.

SIX

STAYING HUMBLE WITH A POSITIVE ATTITUDE

"Humble people are very secure people. They know who they are and don't have to put on airs." - Mother Teresa

ᗆᗆᗆ

Staying humble with a positive attitude is an essential aspect of succeeding in life. Humility is often viewed as a weakness, but it is, in fact, a strength that helps individuals develop a positive attitude, improve their relationships, and achieve success. Several studies have shown that individuals who are humble and positive have better mental and physical health and are more successful in their personal and professional lives.

Imagine you're on the hunt for a new car. You've saved up a good amount of money and want to make sure you're getting the best possible deal for your hard-earned cash. You walk into the first dealership and are greeted by a salesperson who looks like they'd rather be anywhere else but there. They seem annoyed that you've interrupted their day and respond with a curt, "What do you want?" You explain that you're interested in buying a car and ask if they can help you with some information. Instead of being helpful, the salesperson tells you to check the brochures or the website and walks away. You're left feeling frustrated, confused, and completely unimportant. Now, imagine that you walk into another dealership. This time, the salesperson greets you with a warm smile and a friendly "Hello!" You explain that you're interested in buying a car and ask if they can help you with some information. The salesperson listens attentively and asks you some questions to get a better understanding of your needs and budget. They take the time to show you the different models and features available, explain the pros and cons of each option, and answer any questions you have. You never feel rushed or like you're being pressured to buy something you don't want. Instead, you feel like the salesperson genuinely cares about helping you find the right car for you. Which of these experiences would you prefer? Most people would choose the second one. Why? Because people want to be treated with kindness, respect, and humility. They want to feel like their needs and wants matter to the person they're dealing with.

In the world of sales, this is known as customer service. The way a salesperson treats their customers can make or break a sale. But it's not just in sales where being humble and kind is important. It's a critical part of success in all areas of life. A humble person is someone who doesn't think they're better than anyone else. They don't act like they know everything or have all the answers. They're open to learning from others and are willing to admit when they're wrong. They treat everyone with respect, regardless of their job title, income, or status. Why is being humble so important for success? There are several reasons.

Firstly, it helps you build better relationships with others. When you're humble, you're more likely to listen to others and take their perspectives into account. This can lead to better communication, more trust, and stronger connections with the people around you.

Secondly, being humble allows you to learn and grow. If you think you already know everything, you'll never be open to new ideas or ways of thinking. But when you're humble, you recognize that there's always more to learn and that you can benefit from the wisdom and experiences of others.

Thirdly, being humble can help you avoid conflicts and resolve them more easily when they do arise. When you're not focused on proving yourself or being right all the time, you're less likely to get into arguments or disagreements. And when you do find yourself in a conflict, you're more likely to approach it with a level head and a willingness to find a solution that works for everyone involved.

Finally, being humble helps you stay grounded and connected to your values. When you're humble, you don't let success go to your head. You don't get overly confident or cocky. Instead, you stay focused on doing what's right and staying true to who you are. So, if you want to succeed in life, remember the importance of staying humble. Treat others with kindness and respect, be open to learning, and stay true to your values. You'll find that this approach not only leads to success but also to a more fulfilling.

Research has shown that individuals who exhibit humility are more likely to be happy, less anxious, and less stressed. A study published in the Journal of Positive Psychology found that individuals who rated higher on humility measures also had higher levels of life satisfaction and happiness. Humble individuals are more likely to accept their limitations and acknowledge their mistakes, which enables them to learn and grow from their experiences. By maintaining a positive attitude, they can maintain a healthy perspective on their lives and avoid becoming overwhelmed by the challenges they face.

Another study published in the Journal of Personality and Social Psychology found that humble individuals have stronger and more positive relationships with others. Humility is associated with greater empathy and compassion, which helps individuals build stronger connections with others. Additionally, humble individuals are more willing to seek out help and collaborate with others to achieve common goals. This helps them develop stronger relationships, both personally and professionally, that can lead to greater success in the long run.

Maintaining a positive attitude is also essential to achieving success. A study published in the Journal of Happiness Studies found that individuals with a positive attitude have better mental and physical health, are more creative, and are more successful in their personal and professional lives. Positive individuals are more likely to take risks, pursue their goals, and find solutions to problems. They are also more resilient and better able to bounce back from setbacks.

Picture yourself as the salesperson in the story. You're standing at a trade show, showcasing your product to a sea of potential customers. You're feeling confident and positive in the morning, greeting customers with a genuine smile and engaging them in conversation about your product. You feel great about what you're offering, and you can see the customers responding to your enthusiasm. By lunchtime, you've already made several successful sales and generated a lot of interest in your product.

But as the day wears on, you start feeling tired and frustrated. You're no longer feeling as positive as you were in the morning, and you start to doubt yourself and your product. You find yourself greeting customers with a frown and seeming disinterested in their needs. You start to focus more on the limitations of your product and how it's not perfect, rather than on its benefits. As a result, you struggle to make any sales, and customers start avoiding your booth.

This scenario highlights the importance of maintaining a positive attitude, no matter what the circumstances. Your attitude can have a huge impact on your success, both personally and professionally. It's easy to feel positive and confident when things are going well, but it's when the going gets tough that your attitude really matters. The power of positivity is undeniable, and research has shown that a positive attitude can improve your health, increase your productivity, and boost your overall well-being.

In fact, studies have shown that people with a positive attitude are more likely to be successful in all areas of life, including relationships, careers, and personal development. When you maintain a positive attitude, you're more likely to approach challenges with an open mind, and you're better equipped to handle setbacks and obstacles.

On the other hand, a negative attitude can be a self-fulfilling prophecy. When you focus on the negative, you're more likely to experience negative outcomes. Negative thinking can impact your mood, your energy levels, and your ability to think clearly and make sound decisions. It can also impact the way others perceive you, leading to missed opportunities and strained relationships.

So, what can you do to maintain a positive attitude? First, focus on the things that are going well in your life, and try to approach challenges as opportunities for growth and learning. Surround yourself with positive people who uplift and inspire you. Practice self-care by getting enough sleep, eating well, and exercising regularly. Finally, make a conscious effort to shift your perspective and focus on the positive aspects of every situation.

Remember, your attitude is a choice. You can choose to be positive and optimistic, or you can choose to be negative and pessimistic. The choice you make will have a profound impact on your life and your success. Choose positivity, and watch your life and your career flourish.

When we face difficult situations or encounter failures, it is easy to fall into negative thinking patterns and become discouraged. However, maintaining a positive attitude can help us stay motivated and focused on finding solutions to overcome the obstacles in our path.

One of the ways in which a positive attitude helps is by giving us the resilience and mental toughness to bounce back from setbacks. With a positive mindset, we are more likely to view setbacks as temporary and surmountable challenges rather than insurmountable obstacles. We become more willing to learn from our mistakes, make adjustments, and keep moving forward towards our goals.

Another way in which a positive attitude helps is by improving our emotional and mental well-being. Studies have shown that people with positive attitudes tend to have lower levels of stress, anxiety, and depression. They also tend to have better physical health, sleep quality, and overall life satisfaction. This is because a positive attitude fosters a sense of optimism, hope, and gratitude, which can help us stay motivated and resilient in the face of adversity.

Finally, a positive attitude can help us cultivate a growth mindset, which is essential for success. When we have a growth mindset, we believe that our abilities and talents can be developed through hard work and dedication. We view failures as opportunities to learn and grow rather than as evidence of our limitations. This mindset enables us to take risks, embrace challenges, and push beyond our comfort zones, which are all essential for achieving our goals.

To cultivate a positive attitude in the face of setbacks and failures, it is essential to focus on our thoughts and beliefs. We can start by practicing gratitude and focusing on the positive aspects of our lives. We can also reframe negative thoughts and beliefs into more positive ones. For example, instead of thinking, "I can't do this," we can reframe it to "I am capable of overcoming this challenge." It is also important to surround ourselves with positive influences, such as supportive friends and family, and to engage in self-care practices, such as exercise and mindfulness meditation.

A positive attitude is a powerful tool for overcoming setbacks and failures and achieving success in life. It helps us stay motivated, resilient, and focused on finding solutions to overcome obstacles. By cultivating a positive attitude, we can improve our emotional and mental well-being, develop a growth mindset, and achieve our goals.

One example of an individual who has demonstrated the importance of staying humble with a positive attitude is Oprah Winfrey. Despite her immense success, she remains grounded and humble, continually acknowledging her struggles and failures. She attributes her success to her positive attitude, which she says has helped her overcome numerous obstacles throughout her life. Oprah is also known for her philanthropic work, which is a testament to her humble and compassionate nature.

Another example is Mahatma Gandhi, who was known for his humility and positive attitude. Despite being a revolutionary leader, he always maintained a sense of humility and kindness towards others. He believed in the power of positivity and once said, "I will not let anyone walk through my mind with their dirty feet." Gandhi's commitment to his principles and his humble approach to life earned him the respect and admiration of people around the world.

Staying humble with a positive attitude can bring many benefits in life, including gaining respect and admiration from others, improving relationships, and fostering personal growth. Here are some advantages of staying humble:

1. Builds Strong Relationships: When we stay humble, we are able to appreciate and value others for who they are. This helps us build strong relationships and connections with others, as we are not focused on our own egos and needs.

2. Increases Self-Awareness: Staying humble requires us to be self-aware and reflect on our actions and behaviors. This can help us identify areas for improvement and work towards personal growth.

3. Enhances Learning: When we stay humble, we are open to learning from others and accepting feedback. This can help us expand our knowledge and skills, and

ultimately achieve greater success.

4. Improves Reputation: Humble people are often seen as trustworthy, reliable, and respectful. This can enhance our reputation among peers, colleagues, and employers.

Staying positive is another crucial quality for achieving success and happiness. Positive thinking has been shown to have numerous benefits, including improved mood, lower stress levels, and better physical health. A study published in the Journal of Behavioral Medicine found that people who were more optimistic tended to have better immune function and lower rates of cardiovascular disease.

Furthermore, positive thinking helps us to be more resilient in the face of challenges and setbacks. When we maintain a positive attitude, we are more likely to view challenges as opportunities for growth and learning, rather than as insurmountable obstacles. This, in turn, helps us bounce back more quickly from adversity and stay focused on our goals.

So, how can we cultivate a humble and positive attitude in our lives? Here are some tips:

1. Practice Gratitude: Take time each day to reflect on what you are grateful for, and express gratitude to others. This helps us stay grounded and appreciate the positive things in our lives.
2. Seek Feedback: Ask for feedback from others, and be open to constructive criticism. This can help us identify areas for improvement and grow as individuals.
3. Listen to Others: When engaging in conversations, make an effort to listen actively and understand others' perspectives. This helps us learn from others and build stronger relationships.

4. Acknowledge Mistakes: When we make mistakes, it's important to acknowledge them and take responsibility. This shows that we are accountable for our actions and are willing to learn from our mistakes.

5. Celebrate Others' Success: When others succeed, celebrate their achievements and acknowledge their hard work. This helps us stay humble and appreciate the accomplishments of others.

By practicing humility and maintaining a positive attitude, we can not only improve our own lives but also make a positive impact on those around us.

One real-life example of a successful wealthy and humble person is Amancio Ortega, the founder of the fashion brand Zara. Ortega is one of the wealthiest people in the world, but despite his immense success and wealth, he has always remained grounded and focused on his values.

Ortega grew up in a working-class family in Spain and started working in the textile industry at a young age. He worked his way up through the ranks and eventually started his own clothing company, which later became Zara.

Despite his immense wealth, Ortega has always remained humble and focused on his values. He is known for his simple lifestyle and his dedication to his work. He is also known for his generosity and his philanthropy. He has donated millions of dollars to various charitable causes, including cancer research and poverty alleviation.

Ortega is also known for his positive mindset. He has said that he always looks for the good in people and focuses on the positive aspects of life. He believes that having a positive attitude is essential to achieving success in business and in life.

Throughout his career, Ortega has remained true to his values and his humble roots. He is known for his hands-on approach to his business and his dedication to his employees. He is also known for his commitment to sustainability and ethical business practices.

Ortega's success is a testament to the power of hard work, dedication, and a positive mindset. Despite his immense wealth and success, he has never lost sight of what is truly important - his values, his dedication to his work, and his commitment to making a positive impact on the world.

Staying humble can be a powerful tool in battling ego and achieving success in life. Humility is a trait that helps individuals to maintain a realistic and grounded perspective on their abilities and accomplishments. It is a quality that fosters a positive mindset, a growth-oriented approach, and strong relationships with others.

When individuals stay humble, they are less likely to succumb to overconfidence and ego-driven behavior. They understand that their success is not solely the result of their individual efforts, but also the contribution of others around them. They are more likely to respect others' opinions, ideas, and contributions, and less likely to let their own ego take center stage.

Humility also enables individuals to feel happy for others' success. Instead of feeling envious or resentful, humble individuals celebrate others' achievements and view them as sources of inspiration and motivation. This mindset fosters positive relationships and helps to build a supportive community around them.

Staying humble also enables individuals to think with the right mindset. They are less likely to be influenced by negative emotions like jealousy and hatred, which can cloud judgment and lead to poor decision-making. Humility enables individuals to think more objectively and make decisions based on facts and reason, rather than ego or emotion.

When individuals stay humble, they gain respect and appreciation from the people around them. Others are more likely to see them as approachable, kind, and respectful, and to seek out their advice and guidance. This can lead to greater success in both personal and professional relationships.

Many people tend to fall into the trap of arrogance and pride when they achieve small successes. They tend to boast about their accomplishments, basking in the glory of their achievements, and often overlook the fact that these successes are not permanent. They forget that success is a journey and not a destination.

In this regard, it is essential to celebrate small successes but not overdo it or boast about it excessively. Once arrogance and pride are filled in you, they can halt your progress and prevent you from learning and growing. Arrogance creates a sense of "I know everything" attitude, which can become a barrier to acquiring knowledge, learning new things, and making conscious decisions towards growth and success.

The consequences of being arrogant and proud can be severe. People with this attitude tend to be dismissive of others' opinions and ideas, often ignoring their contribution to the team's success. They may also become complacent, thinking that they have already achieved everything they need to and stop working towards their goals.

On the other hand, staying humble with a positive attitude can lead to immense success. Humility allows you to stay open-minded, seek feedback, and learn from others. It allows you to acknowledge your weaknesses and work towards improving them. Staying humble also makes you more approachable, which helps to build strong relationships and a positive work environment.

In conclusion, staying humble with a positive attitude is crucial to achieving long-term success. Pride and arrogance can be detrimental to your progress and prevent you from reaching your full potential. On the other hand, humility allows you to remain open-minded, seek feedback, and learn from others. It creates an ideal environment for growth, fosters positive relationships, and helps to build a successful and fulfilling career.

ᗡᗡᗡ

Brian and Harvey had been colleagues for years, working together in the same company. They had always had a friendly and respectful relationship, and had often collaborated on projects. They both had a positive attitude and a strong work ethic, but what really set them apart was their humility.

Despite their success, they never let it go to their heads. They remained grounded and focused on their work, always striving to improve and learn. They were always willing to help others and give credit where credit was due. They never boasted about their accomplishments, but instead celebrated the success of others.

Their humility and positive attitude had earned them a great reputation within the company. People admired their work ethic and the way they treated others. Their colleagues saw them as approachable and down-to-earth, and often sought out their advice and guidance.

One day, a big project came up that required the expertise of both Brian and Harvey. They were excited to work together again and set to work right away. They approached the project with the same humility and positive attitude that had served them so well in the past.

As they worked on the project, they faced a few setbacks and challenges. But they remained calm and focused, and kept a positive attitude. They worked together to find solutions and overcame each obstacle as it arose.

Their hard work and positive attitude paid off. The project was a huge success, and they received praise from both their colleagues and superiors. But Brian and Harvey never took all the credit for themselves. They thanked their team members and acknowledged the contributions of others.

Their humility and positive attitude not only helped them achieve success, but also earned them the respect and admiration of others. They continued to work hard and stay humble, always striving to learn and grow.

In the end, Brian and Harvey became known as the most successful and well-liked colleagues in the company, all thanks to their humble and positive approach to work and life.

ᕤᕤᕤ

In conclusion, staying humble can be a powerful tool in battling ego, fostering positive relationships, and achieving success in life. It enables individuals to think with the right mindset, respect others, feel happy for others' success, and gain the respect and appreciation of those around them. By cultivating this quality, individuals can expand their horizons, achieve their goals, and build a meaningful and fulfilling life.

here are a few famous people from India and other countries who have been known for their humility and positive mindset:

1. Ratan Tata (India) - He is a well-known Indian industrialist and philanthropist who is known for his humility and grounded personality. Despite being one of the wealthiest individuals in India, he is known for his modesty and his dedication to giving back to society.

2. Satya Nadella (India/USA) - He is the CEO of Microsoft and is known for his humble and approachable personality. He often credits his success to his upbringing and his willingness to learn from others, and he has been praised for his ability to create a positive and inclusive work culture at Microsoft.

3. Roger Federer (Switzerland) - He is one of the greatest tennis players of all time and is known for his humility and sportsmanship. He is often seen congratulating his opponents and acknowledging their efforts, and he has used his success to give back to society through his charitable foundation.

4. Indra Nooyi (India/USA) - She is a former CEO of PepsiCo and is known for her humble and down-to-earth personality. She often speaks about the importance of staying grounded and connected to one's roots, and she has been praised for her leadership and her efforts to create a more sustainable and socially responsible business model.

5. Sachin Tendulkar (India) - He is a former cricketer and is known for his humility and dedication to the sport. Despite being one of the greatest cricketers of all time, he has always maintained a modest and unassuming personality, and he has used his success to inspire others and give back to society through his charitable foundation.

These individuals have demonstrated that success and humility can go hand in hand, and that one does not have to compromise on their values or principles to achieve greatness. They serve as role models for others and inspire us to stay humble, stay positive, and strive for excellence in all that we do.

A positive mindset is an essential element for success and happiness in life. It is a way of thinking that allows us to focus on our strengths, opportunities, and possibilities, rather than dwelling on our weaknesses, obstacles, and limitations. Having a positive mindset means that we are able to approach challenges with optimism and resilience, and that we are more likely to find solutions and opportunities even in the face of adversity.

On the other hand, if we do not have a positive mindset, we may find ourselves stuck in a cycle of negativity, self-doubt, and fear. We may become overwhelmed by our problems, and may feel helpless or powerless to overcome them. This negative mindset can lead to stress, anxiety, and depression, and can have a negative impact on our relationships, our work, and our overall well-being.

So why is it important to cultivate a positive mindset? There are many reasons. For one, a positive mindset can help us to be more resilient and adaptable in the face of change and uncertainty. It can help us to see setbacks as opportunities for growth, and to learn from our mistakes rather than dwelling on them. A positive mindset can also help us to build stronger relationships with others, as we are more likely to see the best in others and to communicate in a constructive and empathetic way.

Additionally, a positive mindset can help us to achieve our goals and dreams. When we approach our goals with optimism and confidence, we are more likely to take action and to persist in the face of challenges. This can lead to greater success and fulfillment in our personal and professional lives.

So how can we cultivate a positive mindset? Here are a few tips:

1. Focus on gratitude: Take time each day to reflect on the things that you are grateful for. This can help you to shift your focus from what you don't have to what you do have, and can help you to cultivate a more positive outlook on life.
2. Practice positive self-talk: Be mindful of the language that you use when you talk to yourself. Replace negative self-talk with positive affirmations, and try to focus on your strengths and abilities rather than your weaknesses.
3. Surround yourself with positivity: Surround yourself with people who uplift and inspire you, and seek out positive experiences and environments. This can help to reinforce your positive mindset and to counteract negative influences.
4. Take care of your physical health: Your physical health can have a big impact on your mental health. Make sure that you are getting enough sleep, eating a healthy diet, and engaging in regular exercise.
5. Embrace failure: Don't be afraid to fail. Embrace failure as an opportunity to learn and grow, and use it as motivation to keep moving forward.

In conclusion, a positive mindset is a key ingredient for success and happiness in life. By cultivating a positive outlook and taking steps to nurture our mental health and well-being, we can build resilience, achieve our goals, and live a more fulfilling and satisfying life.

Staying humble is not only about being modest and respectful towards others, but it also saves us from falling into the trap of trying to impress others. When we are constantly trying to impress others with our skills, education, or accomplishments, we are essentially seeking validation from external sources. While there is nothing wrong with being proud of our achievements, seeking validation from others can lead to a never-ending cycle of trying to impress others, which can be exhausting and unfulfilling.

Moreover, the need to impress others can also lead to the creation of a false persona, where we present an idealized version of ourselves to others, rather than being our true selves. This false persona can be difficult to maintain and can cause us to feel disconnected from our true selves. It can also be tiring to constantly try to keep up appearances, leading to stress and burnout.

In contrast, when we stay humble, we focus on our own growth and development rather than seeking validation from others. We work on our skills and education because we value self-improvement, not because we want to impress others. This leads to a more authentic and fulfilling life, where we are true to ourselves and not trying to maintain a false face.

Additionally, staying humble also allows us to appreciate the achievements of others without feeling threatened or envious. When we are not constantly trying to impress others, we are more likely to be happy for the success of others rather than feeling envious or competitive. This positive attitude towards others can lead to more fulfilling and meaningful relationships, both personally and professionally.

In summary, staying humble saves us from the never-ending cycle of trying to impress others for validation and helps us to stay true to ourselves. It also allows us to appreciate the achievements of others and fosters positive relationships. So, rather than focusing on impressing others, let us focus on our own growth and development, and live an authentic and fulfilling life.

ᗰᗰᗰ

Chapter Summary:

In this chapter, we explored the significance of cultivating a positive mindset and maintaining humility as crucial factors for success in life. Despite humility often being perceived as a weakness, it was revealed to be a strength that facilitated the development of a positive attitude, improved relationships, and ultimately led to achievements.

Several studies were cited, indicating that individuals who displayed humility and positivity experienced better mental and physical health while achieving success in their personal and professional lives. The Journal of Positive Psychology published a study demonstrating that individuals who scored higher on humility measures also reported increased levels of life satisfaction and happiness. By accepting their limitations and acknowledging mistakes, humble individuals were able to learn and grow from their experiences. This enabled them to maintain a healthy perspective on life and avoid becoming overwhelmed by challenges.

Furthermore, the Journal of Personality and Social Psychology presented research findings that emphasized the positive impact of humility on relationships. Humble individuals exhibited greater empathy and compassion, which strengthened their connections with others. Their willingness to seek help and collaborate with others for common goals fostered stronger personal and professional relationships, leading to long-term success.

A positive attitude proved beneficial in multiple ways. It provided individuals with resilience and mental toughness to rebound from setbacks. With a positive mindset, obstacles were perceived as temporary challenges rather than insurmountable barriers. Mistakes were seen as opportunities for growth, allowing for adjustments and continued progress towards goals.

Moreover, maintaining a positive attitude contributed to emotional and mental well-being. Studies demonstrated that individuals with positive mindsets experienced lower levels of stress, anxiety, and depression. They also enjoyed better physical health, quality of sleep, and overall life satisfaction. Optimism, hope, and gratitude cultivated through a positive attitude empowered individuals to stay motivated and resilient in the face of adversity.

Lastly, a positive attitude enabled the cultivation of a growth mindset, an essential element for success. Those with a growth mindset believed in the development of their abilities and talents through hard work and dedication. Failures were viewed as learning opportunities rather than limitations. This mindset encouraged risk-taking, embracing challenges, and pushing beyond comfort zones, all crucial for achieving goals.

Activity: Cultivating Humility and a Positive Mindset

1. *Reflection: Take some time each day to reflect on your actions, thoughts, and interactions. Ask yourself if you approached situations with humility and a positive mindset. Identify areas where you can improve and set goals for practicing humility and positivity.*
2. *Gratitude Journal: Start a gratitude journal and write down three things you are grateful for each day. This exercise helps shift your focus towards the positive aspects of your life, fostering a grateful and optimistic mindset.*
3. *Empathy Exercise: Engage in activities that promote empathy and understanding. Volunteer at a local charity or spend time listening to others without judgment. Practice putting yourself in someone else's shoes to develop empathy and a deeper appreciation for diverse perspectives.*
4. *Acknowledge Mistakes: When you make a mistake, acknowledge it openly and take responsibility. Practice self-reflection and learn from these experiences, allowing them to shape your growth and development. Embrace the opportunity to apologize and make amends when necessary.*
5. *Positive Affirmations: Incorporate positive affirmations into your daily routine. Repeat empowering statements about yourself and your abilities, reinforcing a positive self-image and mindset. For example, say, "I am capable and deserving of success" or "I approach challenges with a positive attitude."*
6. *Seek Feedback: Regularly seek feedback from trusted individuals in your personal and professional life. Be open to constructive criticism and use it as an opportunity for growth. Actively listen and consider different perspectives,*

fostering a humble and receptive mindset.

7. *Random Acts of Kindness: Engage in random acts of kindness to spread positivity and humility. Perform simple acts of kindness, such as holding the door for someone, offering compliments, or assisting someone in need. These actions not only benefit others but also cultivate a sense of gratitude and humility within yourself.*

8. *Mindfulness and Meditation: Practice mindfulness and meditation to cultivate awareness and a calm, positive mindset. Set aside a few minutes each day to focus on your breath, observe your thoughts without judgment, and cultivate a sense of peace and gratitude.*

9. *Surround Yourself with Positive Influences: Evaluate the people and media you surround yourself with. Seek out positive influences, whether through books, podcasts, or supportive individuals who uplift and inspire you. Surrounding yourself with positivity can help reinforce a positive mindset and humility.*

Remember, cultivating humility and a positive mindset is an ongoing process. Be patient with yourself and commit to these activities consistently. Over time, you will develop a habit of staying humble and embracing a positive attitude in all aspects of your life.

❦❦❦

SEVEN

HONESTY AND TRUTH: THE CORNERSTONE OF SUCCESS

❧

ᗡᗡᗡ

"Truth never damages a cause that is just." -
Mahatma Gandhi.

ᗡᗡᗡ

It was my first job and I was still getting used to the corporate world. I had set my alarm the previous night, but when it rang in the morning, I hit the snooze button a few too many times. Before I knew it, I was running late for work.

As I rushed into the elevator, I saw my boss's boss standing there with a cup of coffee in his hand. It was the super boss, the man who oversaw all the departments in the company. My heart sank. I knew that being late was a serious offense in the corporate world and I feared that I would be reprimanded.

To my surprise, when my super boss addressed me, he simply asked, "Did you arrive late to work?" Caught off guard, I couldn't bring myself to fabricate a story, so I mustered the courage to tell him the truth. "Yes, I'm truly sorry. I overslept." To my amazement, my super boss responded with a warm smile and shared a valuable insight. "Honesty and truthfulness are priceless virtues in this world. They are not easily found in everyone." He expressed his satisfaction with my straightforwardness, admitting that he had half-expected me to blame traffic or come up with other excuses. His words resonated deeply with me.

This encounter served as a gentle reminder of the importance of humility and honesty in my life. Although I have always held these values close to my heart, hearing them emphasized by someone of such high stature in the corporate world was truly humbling. It reinforced my belief that genuine honesty is a trait to be cherished and nurtured, as it fosters trust and genuine connections with others. In a world where shortcuts and deceit can often be tempting, this encounter reaffirmed my commitment to always remain true to myself and others.

From that day on, my super boss started talking to me every day. He would share his experiences and insights with me, and I would listen intently, soaking up all the knowledge I could. As someone from an Indian Navy background, I couldn't have found a more suitable mentor.

This profound incident served as a powerful lesson, revealing the vital significance of honesty and integrity within the corporate world and beyond. It unveiled to me the remarkable appreciation people hold for those who embody transparency and truthfulness in their interactions. Above all, it instilled in me a profound appreciation for the role of mentors and the immeasurable value of learning from individuals who possess greater wisdom and experience.

Looking back on that day, I am grateful for the lesson that my super boss taught me.

There was another such incident a few years later when I had moved to a different company, I vividly remember a time when my honesty was put to the test, and it ended up being the very thing that won me a valuable client. It was a few years back, and I was working as a consultant at a multinational company. I was tasked with handling the technical aspects of a project that involved a particularly demanding and aggressive client.

Now, my colleague who was responsible for managing the client's business requirements had taken personal leave to attend his brother's wedding, leaving me to handle the client all by myself. And just my luck, the client demanded that we shorten the deadline, insisting that the project be completed sooner than what had been committed to.

Without missing a beat, I responded with honesty and transparency, telling the client that I wasn't entirely sure what commitments had been made previously, but that based on the project's requirements, it could only be delivered on a later date than my colleague had committed. Unfortunately, my honesty wasn't received well, and the client was furious. He escalated the issue to my boss, and the next thing I knew, my boss and I were on a flight to another city to pacify the client.

During the flight, my boss kept telling me that I needed to learn to be more diplomatic and less upfront with my honesty. I reluctantly agreed, but as time went on, I realized that being honest had won me something much more valuable than mere diplomacy.

Despite not being able to deliver the project on the timeline my boss and colleague had committed, we were able to complete it a day earlier than the timeline I had provided.

The client's initial reaction to my honesty had left me feeling doubtful about whether or not I had made the right choice. But as it turned out, my transparency had won me a great deal more than I could have ever imagined.

After we finally delivered the project, the client's attitude towards me had completely shifted. He went from being angry and frustrated to expressing his admiration for my honesty and integrity. From that day on, he made it a point to work with me on all future projects, and he even went as far as ensuring that he took timelines from me directly rather than going through my boss.

The client's newfound faith in me was a testament to the fact that honesty truly does pay off. It had taken a bit of drama and a lot of perseverance, but in the end, my integrity had won me a valuable client who ended up becoming a good friend.

Over the next four years, we worked together on multiple projects, and with each passing day, our partnership grew stronger. We achieved some incredible milestones together, and the client's trust in my abilities continued to grow.

Looking back on that incident now, I can't help but smile at how things had turned out. If it weren't for that moment of honesty, I might have never earned the trust and respect of one of the most demanding clients I had ever worked with. And while it wasn't always easy, it was worth it to know that my integrity had made all the difference.

I want to clarify that the story I shared earlier is just a small example of how honesty can sometimes work in our favor. I am fully aware that my experience pales in comparison to the incredible feats achieved by great leaders like Gandhi and Washington. I don't want to sound like I am trying to elevate myself to their level in any way.

My intent in sharing this story was simply to highlight the importance of honesty in our daily lives and how it can help build trust and strong relationships, even in the most challenging situations. I believe that if we all strive to be honest and transparent in our interactions with others, we can make a positive impact on the world around us, no matter how small it may be.

So please don't mistake my story for anything more than a humble account of my own personal experience, I am also sure that you many of you reading this have had your own personal experiences with honesty and integrity.

Honesty is the foundation of any successful and fulfilling life. It is the cornerstone of personal integrity and the basis for all healthy relationships, both with ourselves and others. Yet, we often find ourselves struggling to be honest with ourselves, especially when it comes to our own shortcomings and failures.

The first step towards achieving honesty with oneself is to recognize the voice within that warns us when we are not being truthful. We all have that inner voice that calls us out when we indulge in our weaknesses, such as overeating or procrastinating. However, many of us choose to ignore that voice, preferring to make excuses or shift the blame onto external factors. It is important to listen to that voice, to acknowledge our weaknesses and mistakes, and to take responsibility for our actions.

When we are honest with ourselves, we can start to strengthen our sense of self-awareness and develop a greater understanding of our values and goals. This, in turn, can help us to become more focused and dedicated towards our pursuits, and to make more deliberate and thoughtful decisions.

However, being honest with oneself is easier said than done. It requires a deep level of self-reflection and introspection, which can be uncomfortable and even painful at times. It requires us to confront our fears, weaknesses, and failures head-on, and to take responsibility for them. This can be a difficult process, but it is also an essential one.

Once we have achieved honesty with ourselves, we can start to extend that honesty towards others. Being honest with others can be a challenging task, as it often requires us to confront difficult situations and have uncomfortable conversations. However, by being truthful and transparent with others, we can build stronger and more meaningful relationships, based on mutual trust and respect.

In his autobiography, "The Story of My Experiments with Truth," Mahatma Gandhi describes his unwavering commitment to honesty with self and others. Gandhi believed that honesty was the cornerstone of all moral and spiritual progress and that one could not truly make progress without first being honest with oneself. Throughout the book, Gandhi shares examples of times when he struggled with his own sense of honesty, particularly during his youth when he used to steal coins from his brother. He realized that this behavior was dishonest and unethical, and he made a conscious effort to change it.

Gandhi's commitment to honesty extended to all aspects of his life, including his political and social activism. He believed that the fight for Indian independence must be based on truth and nonviolence, and he refused to use any means that he deemed dishonest or violent. Gandhi's belief in the power of honesty and nonviolence eventually led to India's independence from British colonial rule.

Numerous studies have shown that practicing honesty with oneself can have a positive impact on mental and emotional well-being. For instance, a 2012 study published in the Journal of Personality and Social Psychology found that people who lied less frequently reported better physical and mental health than those who lied more often. Additionally, being honest with oneself can lead to greater self-awareness and personal growth. As Gandhi's life demonstrates, a commitment to honesty can have a profound impact on one's life and the lives of those around them.

Mahatma Gandhi is widely regarded as one of the greatest leaders in Indian history. One of the key pillars of his leadership philosophy was the unwavering commitment to honesty and truth. Throughout his life, Gandhi remained steadfast in his belief that these values were essential to achieving success not only in one's personal life but also in the realm of politics and social reform.

Gandhi's commitment to honesty and truth was evident from a very young age. As a student in London, he lived a simple life, subsisting on a vegetarian diet and refusing to indulge in materialistic pursuits. He was honest with himself and with others about his beliefs and values, even when they differed from those around him. This commitment to truth continued throughout his life, as he refused to compromise on his principles, even in the face of great adversity.

One of the most famous examples of Gandhi's commitment to honesty and truth occurred during his time as a lawyer in South Africa. At the time, South Africa was under British colonial rule, and discrimination against non-white people was rampant. Gandhi became involved in the struggle for Indian rights, and his activism eventually led to his arrest and imprisonment. While in jail, Gandhi was visited by a high-ranking British official who tried to persuade him to abandon his cause in exchange for his freedom. Gandhi refused, stating that he could not compromise on his beliefs, even if it meant remaining in prison.

Gandhi's commitment to honesty and truth extended beyond his personal life and activism. He believed that these values were essential to achieving success in politics and social reform. Throughout his career, Gandhi worked tirelessly to promote his vision of a just and equal society, one in which everyone had equal rights and opportunities. He was able to inspire millions of people to join him in this fight by remaining honest and true to his principles, even in the face of great opposition.

Gandhi's commitment to honesty and truth had a profound impact on the course of Indian history. His unwavering commitment to these values inspired millions of people to join the struggle for independence, leading to the eventual end of British colonial rule. Gandhi's example also inspired leaders around the world to adopt similar values in their own struggles for social justice and equality.

In conclusion, Mahatma Gandhi's commitment to honesty and truth was a cornerstone of his success as a leader and a social reformer. His unwavering commitment to these values inspired millions of people to join him in the struggle for justice and equality. Gandhi's example shows us that honesty and truth are not just moral values, but also essential tools for achieving success in our personal and professional lives. By remaining true to our principles and being honest with ourselves and others, we can achieve our goals and make a positive impact on the world around us.

One of the most famous stories of honesty and truth is that of George Washington and the cherry tree. The story goes that as a young boy, Washington received a hatchet as a gift and proceeded to chop down one of his father's cherry trees. When his father discovered the tree had been cut down, he asked his son if he had done it. Rather than denying his actions or blaming someone else, Washington replied, "I cannot tell a lie, I did cut it with my hatchet." This admission of guilt earned Washington the respect and admiration of his father, and became a symbol of his honesty and integrity throughout his life.

Patagonia's commitment to environmental sustainability and social responsibility has earned them a reputation for honesty and transparency. The "Don't Buy This Jacket" campaign, in particular, demonstrated their willingness to prioritize their values over profits. By urging consumers to think twice before buying new clothes, Patagonia showed that they were not just interested in selling more products, but were also committed to reducing waste and encouraging sustainable consumption.

In addition to their campaigns, Patagonia has also taken several steps to reduce their environmental impact. They have implemented a "Worn Wear" program, where customers can bring in their old Patagonia gear to be repaired or recycled. They have also made significant investments in renewable energy and have implemented sustainable sourcing practices for their materials.

By being transparent about their practices and demonstrating a commitment to their values, Patagonia has built a loyal customer base that shares their values. In fact, a 2018 survey found that 67% of Patagonia customers said they were more likely to buy from the company because of its social and environmental commitments. This is a testament to the power of honesty and transparency in building trust and loyalty with customers.

Honesty is indeed a powerful tool that can transform the world into a paradise. The impact of honesty can be felt in every aspect of our lives, from personal relationships to global conflicts. When we stay honest with ourselves and others, we create a foundation of trust and respect that can solve many of the world's problems.

In the case of border conflicts, many of them arise from a lack of transparency and honesty. If nations and leaders were honest about their intentions and interests, it would be easier to find common ground and work towards peaceful resolutions. When leaders prioritize honesty and transparency, it creates an environment where trust can thrive, and cooperation becomes easier.

Similarly, in the business world, brands that prioritize transparency and honesty over profits are more likely to succeed in the long run. Customers appreciate brands that are honest about their products, their manufacturing processes, and their impact on the environment. When brands prioritize customer comfort over profits, they create a loyal customer base that supports their growth and expansion.

Honesty in education can also have a transformative effect on society. If teachers are honest with their students about the value of education and the importance of hard work, it can inspire students to become lifelong learners and achieve their full potential. Similarly, if students are honest about their strengths and weaknesses, they can receive the help they need to succeed and grow.

Finally, in personal relationships, honesty is the key to building trust and deep connections with others. When we are honest with our loved ones, we create an environment of trust and mutual respect that allows us to grow together and support each other through life's ups and downs.

Everlane, a clothing company that prides itself on "radical transparency."Everlane's commitment to transparency has been a major factor in their success. By providing detailed information about their products and production processes, they have built a strong reputation for honesty and integrity with their customers. This has helped them to establish a loyal customer base who appreciates their commitment to sustainability, ethical production, and fair pricing.

Everlane's transparency has also helped them to differentiate themselves from other clothing brands. In an industry where fast fashion and cheap labor are common practices, Everlane's commitment to ethical production and transparency has resonated with consumers who are increasingly concerned about the impact of their purchases on the environment and on workers.

In addition to building a strong reputation for transparency, Everlane has also been successful in leveraging their transparency to drive sales. By providing detailed information about their products and pricing, they have been able to create a sense of trust with their customers, which has translated into increased sales and brand loyalty.

Overall, Everlane's commitment to transparency has been a key factor in their success. By being open and honest with their customers, they have been able to establish a strong reputation for integrity and build a loyal customer base that values sustainability, ethical production, and fair pricing.

While some historians believe that the cherry tree story may be apocryphal, there are countless other examples of individuals who have demonstrated honesty and truth in their lives.

Beautycounter's commitment to honesty and transparency has helped the brand gain a loyal following. In an industry where there is a lack of regulation and transparency around ingredients used in personal care products, Beautycounter's transparency is refreshing and reassuring for consumers. By disclosing all of the ingredients used in their products and creating a list of ingredients they won't use, they empower consumers to make informed choices about the products they use on their skin.

Beautycounter's focus on safer ingredients also sets them apart from many other beauty brands. With growing concerns about the potential health risks associated with certain ingredients commonly used in personal care products, many consumers are looking for safer alternatives. Beautycounter's commitment to using safer ingredients provides a clear value proposition for consumers who prioritize their health and wellness.

Additionally, Beautycounter's transparency extends beyond their products to their business practices. They are committed to ethical sourcing and fair labor practices, and they disclose information about their supply chain and manufacturing processes. By being transparent about their business practices, they build trust with consumers and differentiate themselves from other beauty brands.

Overall, Beautycounter's commitment to honesty and transparency has helped the brand build a strong reputation for integrity and trustworthiness. In a crowded and often confusing marketplace, their transparency provides consumers with the information they need to make informed choices and feel confident in their purchases.

In today's world, it is unfortunate that honesty is often overlooked in favor of greed, power, and money. However, there are still companies and individuals who prioritize honesty and integrity over profit and personal gain. These organizations and leaders set an example for the rest of us to follow and inspire us to strive for honesty in our own lives.

By incorporating honesty as a policy, these organizations and individuals demonstrate that it is possible to be successful without sacrificing one's values and integrity. They prove that honesty and transparency can actually be beneficial for business, as it leads to trust and loyalty from customers and stakeholders.

In our personal lives, honesty is equally important. It takes courage and strength to be honest with ourselves and others, but doing so can lead to personal growth and success. When we are honest with ourselves, we are better able to identify our strengths and weaknesses and make decisions that align with our values and goals. Being honest with others builds trust and strengthens relationships, both personally and professionally.

If we all strive to incorporate honesty into our daily lives, we can contribute towards creating a more wonderful society. When we are honest with ourselves and others, we can communicate effectively, collaborate with others, and work towards common goals. We can build a world where people are respected for their honesty and integrity, and where we can trust and rely on each other.

Tips for practicing honesty and truth in daily life:

1. Always speak the truth, even if it is uncomfortable or difficult.
2. Avoid exaggerating or embellishing the truth for personal gain.
3. Be honest with yourself about your strengths and weaknesses.
4. Admit your mistakes and take responsibility for your actions.
5. Be transparent in your dealings with others, whether in personal or professional settings.
6. Avoid compromising on your principles for personal gain or advancement.
7. Surround yourself with people who share your commitment to honesty and truth.
8. Continuously evaluate your actions and decisions to ensure they align with your values

ϸϸϸ

Chapter Summary:

In this chapter, we explored the profound impact of honesty and truthfulness in our lives. Through personal anecdotes and examples, we witnessed how honesty can lead to unexpected opportunities and foster genuine connections. We learned that being honest with ourselves is the first step towards personal growth and self-awareness. By acknowledging our weaknesses and taking responsibility for our actions, we can make deliberate and thoughtful decisions. The stories of Mahatma Gandhi and George Washington showcased how honesty and truth were foundational to their leadership and societal impact. We also examined the role of honesty in organizations, as demonstrated by Patagonia's commitment to transparency and environmental sustainability. Ultimately, we discovered that honesty is a powerful tool that can transform relationships, resolve conflicts, and create a foundation of trust in our personal and professional lives. By embracing honesty and truthfulness, we can make a positive impact on the world around us and foster a more harmonious and authentic society.

Activity:

1. *Reflective Journaling: Take some time to reflect on your own level of honesty and truthfulness in different areas of your life. Write down instances where you have been tempted to be dishonest and how it made you feel. Consider areas where you can improve your honesty and truthfulness.*

2. *Accountability Partner: Find a trusted friend or family member who can serve as your accountability partner. Share your commitment to cultivating honesty and truthfulness habits with them. Ask them to check in with you*

periodically and provide support and encouragement.

3. *Daily Affirmations: Create a list of positive affirmations related to honesty and truthfulness. Repeat these affirmations to yourself every morning or whenever you need a reminder. Believe in your ability to be honest and truthful in all aspects of your life.*

4. *Practice Transparency: Identify a situation or relationship where you can practice being more transparent. Make a conscious effort to share your thoughts, feelings, and intentions openly. Embrace vulnerability and strive for open communication with others.*

5. *Mindful Decision-Making: Before making important decisions, pause and reflect on the values of honesty and truthfulness. Consider the potential consequences of your choices and how they align with these values. Let honesty and truthfulness guide your decision-making process.*

6. *Gratitude Journal: Start a gratitude journal and write down three things you are grateful for each day. Include moments where you acted with honesty and truthfulness. Cultivate gratitude for the opportunities to be honest and the positive impact it has on your life and relationships.*

Remember, cultivating honesty and truthfulness habits is a journey that requires practice and self-reflection. These activities will help you develop and reinforce these important virtues in your daily life.

ᑭᑭᑭ

EIGHT

PUNCTUALITY AND ETHICS: THE BASIS OF PROFESSIONALISM

"Remember that time is money." - Benjamin Franklin

ᚦᚦᚦ

Punctuality and ethics are essential qualities necessary for success in any endeavor. Punctuality demonstrates a respect for time and other people's schedules, while ethics involve doing what is right, even when no one is watching. When combined, these qualities create a foundation of integrity that inspires trust and respect from others. When people are punctual and ethical, they are viewed as reliable and dependable, and this reputation can open doors for opportunities that might not have been available otherwise. Punctuality and ethics can also create a positive environment that fosters productivity, efficiency, and teamwork. When everyone shows up on time and does what they say they will do, projects are completed on schedule, and goals are achieved. Furthermore, when people behave ethically, they build trust with others, which can lead to lasting relationships, both personal and professional. Punctuality and ethics are two critical ingredients for success, and anyone who wants to succeed in life must cultivate these qualities.

One individual whose story epitomizes punctuality is Sir Sandford Fleming. Born in Scotland in 1827, he later moved to Canada in 1845 and became involved in various engineering projects, including the construction of the Intercolonial Railway, which connected Nova Scotia and New Brunswick.

Fleming is widely known as the "Father of Standard Time" for his significant contribution to the development of the worldwide standard time zone system. From his early days as a young apprentice, Fleming displayed an unwavering commitment to punctuality. He consistently arrived at work precisely at 6:00 AM, an hour before his official shift began, despite facing reprimands from his boss. Fleming believed punctuality demonstrated self-respect and respect for others.

Throughout his life, Fleming's dedication to punctuality remained steadfast. As a surveyor for the Canadian Pacific Railway, he played a pivotal role in coordinating the construction of the first transcontinental railroad across Canada. His commitment to punctuality deepened when he missed a train due to a scheduling error. This incident motivated him to develop a standardized system of timekeeping to prevent such errors. In 1876, Fleming presented his proposal for a worldwide standard time system at the Royal Canadian Institute in Toronto. The proposal gained acceptance and was implemented in many countries.

Fleming's commitment to punctuality became even more evident when he missed a train due to a scheduling error. Motivated by this incident, he embarked on developing a standardized system of timekeeping that would prevent such errors in the future. In 1876, Fleming presented his proposal for a worldwide standard time system at a meeting of the Royal Canadian Institute in Toronto. This proposal eventually gained acceptance and was implemented in many countries worldwide.

In 1884, Fleming was appointed as the chair of the International Prime Meridian Conference, which was tasked with standardizing the world's time zones. At the time, each country and even each city had its own unique system of time, which made international travel and communication difficult. Fleming proposed a system in which the world would be divided into 24 equal time zones, each one hour apart, with the prime meridian (which runs through Greenwich, England) serving as the reference point for time. The proposal was adopted and implemented on November 18, 1883.

Fleming's contributions extended beyond timekeeping. He played a vital role in the construction of the transatlantic telegraph cable, connecting North America and Europe. To ensure accurate timing of transmissions, he proposed the use of a universal time standard based on Greenwich Mean Time.

But Fleming's commitment to punctuality did not end there. He was determined to ensure that everyone in

Canada was aware of the new time zone system and the importance of punctuality. He proposed that all railway stations and public clocks should be synchronized to the new standard time, and he developed a system of distributing time signals across the country using telegraph wires.

On January 1, 1884, Fleming's system went into effect. At precisely noon, the time signals were sent out across the country, and all public clocks were reset to the new standard time. It was a remarkable achievement, and it marked the beginning of a new era in timekeeping.

Sir Sandford Fleming's story serves as an exceptional testament to the importance of punctuality. His unwavering commitment to being on time and respecting the schedules of others has left a lasting impact on the world. Fleming's legacy reminds us that punctuality is not merely a matter of being on time but also a demonstration of respect for others. His story inspires us to embrace punctuality as a reflection of our character and a way to honor the time of those around us.

Fleming's commitment to punctuality continued to be evident in his personal life as well. He was known to arrive early for appointments and meetings, and he was never late. In fact, he once arrived at a meeting of the Royal Society of Canada so early that he had to wait outside for an hour before the doors were unlocked.

Fleming's commitment to punctuality was not just about being on time for the sake of being on time. He believed that punctuality was a sign of respect for others and a reflection of one's own character. He once said, "Punctuality is not only a duty, but is also a part of good manners; it is favorable to fortune, reputation, influence, and usefulness; a little attention and energy will form the habit, so as to make it easy and delightful."

Sir Sandford Fleming's story is a testament to the power of punctuality. His unwavering commitment to being on time and respecting the schedules of others had a profound impact on the development of the worldwide time zone system and set a standard for punctuality that is still admired today. Sir Sandford Fleming's story is a shining example of the importance of punctuality. His dedication to developing a standardized time system and his personal commitment to punctuality have had a lasting impact on the world. His legacy reminds us that punctuality is not just about being on time but also about respecting the time of others. As Fleming himself once said, "Time is the very soul of business."

Japan is renowned for its cultural values and practices, and one of its most notable aspects is a strong commitment to punctuality. In Japan, being on time is considered a significant indicator of respect and professionalism. The Japanese people hold punctuality in high regard, and being late is viewed as a sign of disrespect and unprofessionalism.

Highest level of commitment to punctuality can be seen in Japan's public transportation system. Trains in Japan are known for being incredibly punctual, with an average delay of just 18 seconds. This level of punctuality is achieved through a variety of measures, including advanced technology and a strong sense of accountability.

For instance, train conductors in Japan are responsible for keeping their trains on schedule, and they take this responsibility very seriously. They use a system called "jikokuhyo," which means "timetable," to ensure that they are always on time. This system includes a detailed schedule that outlines the exact time the train should arrive and depart at each station, and conductors are expected to stick to this schedule as closely as possible.

Furthermore, Japanese commuters are also committed to punctuality. They plan their journeys carefully and leave plenty of time to ensure they arrive at their destination on time. This commitment to punctuality is not limited to public transportation, but is also reflected in Japanese business culture, where being late for a meeting or appointment is seen as a serious breach of etiquette.

In Japan, punctuality is not just about being on time, but also about demonstrating respect for others and a commitment to professionalism. It is a cultural value that is deeply ingrained in the Japanese mindset and contributes to the efficiency and productivity of their society as a whole.

Punctuality is not only about being on time for appointments, but it extends to other aspects of life such as career, relationships, and self-commitment. Being punctual in these areas can have a significant impact on one's personal and professional growth. In this essay, we will explore why punctuality is important in all areas of life and what happens if one is not punctual.

Career: Punctuality is a critical aspect of a successful career. Showing up on time for work, meetings, and deadlines demonstrates reliability and respect for colleagues and superiors. It also helps to establish a positive reputation and can lead to increased opportunities and advancement. Conversely, being consistently late or missing deadlines can damage professional relationships, impact productivity, and hinder career growth. For example, if an employee frequently misses deadlines, it can create stress for colleagues and impact the overall success of the team.

Relationships: Punctuality is equally important in personal relationships. Being punctual shows respect for others and demonstrates reliability, which is vital for building trust and strengthening relationships. Whether it's meeting friends, family, or romantic partners, being on time shows that you value their time and that you are committed to the relationship. On the other hand, being consistently late or canceling plans last minute can damage trust and negatively impact the relationship. For example, if you are always late for a date or meeting with friends, they may feel like you do not value their time or prioritize the relationship.

Self-commitment: Punctuality is also important when it comes to self-commitment. Whether it's setting goals or completing tasks, being punctual helps to establish a sense of discipline and motivation. By setting deadlines and adhering to them, one can develop a sense of achievement and build self-confidence. Conversely, consistently missing deadlines or failing to commit to goals can damage self-esteem and hinder personal growth. For example, if you set a goal to exercise every day, but consistently skip workouts, it can damage your self-esteem and prevent you from achieving your fitness goals.

Overall, being punctual in all aspects of life is important for personal and professional growth. It shows respect for others and builds trust, which is critical for success in both personal and professional relationships. Additionally, punctuality helps to establish a sense of discipline and motivation, which is vital for achieving personal goals and developing self-confidence.

In contrast, not being punctual can have serious consequences. It can damage professional relationships, impact productivity, and hinder career growth. It can also damage personal relationships and prevent the development of meaningful connections. Failing to commit to personal goals or consistently missing deadlines can damage self-esteem and prevent personal growth.

Punctuality is not only important when it comes to time management but extends to all aspects of life, including career, relationships, and self-commitment. Being punctual shows respect for others, builds trust, and establishes a sense of discipline and motivation, which is critical for personal and professional growth. Failing to be punctual can have serious consequences, damaging relationships and hindering personal and professional growth. Therefore, it is essential to prioritize punctuality and make a conscious effort to be on time in all aspects of life. By doing so, you can build strong relationships, achieve personal goals, and achieve success in all areas of life.

Adopting punctuality in life can be a challenging process, but it is essential for personal and professional success. Here are some ways an individual can adopt punctuality:

Understand the importance of punctuality: Recognize that being punctual shows respect for others and demonstrates reliability. It also helps to establish a positive reputation and can lead to increased opportunities and advancement.

1. Assess your current habits: Take a look at your current habits and identify areas where you struggle with punctuality. Do you tend to run late for appointments or miss deadlines? Knowing your weaknesses will help you develop a plan for improvement.
2. Set realistic goals: Set realistic goals for yourself and establish a timeline for achieving them. For example, if

you typically arrive late for work, set a goal to arrive 10 minutes early each day for a week.

3. Create a schedule: Create a schedule and stick to it. This will help you stay on track and make sure you have enough time to complete tasks and arrive on time for appointments.
4. Use technology: Use technology to help you stay on track. Set reminders and alarms to keep you focused and on time.
5. Hold yourself accountable: Take responsibility for your actions and hold yourself accountable for being punctual. If you do run late, apologize and make amends.
6. Practice discipline: Adopt a mindset of discipline and motivation. Set deadlines and adhere to them, even if it means sacrificing other activities.
7. Celebrate successes: Celebrate your successes and recognize the progress you have made. This will help you stay motivated and committed to your goals.

In conclusion, adopting punctuality in life requires a conscious effort and a commitment to change. By understanding the importance of punctuality, assessing current habits, setting realistic goals, creating a schedule, using technology, holding oneself accountable, practicing discipline, and celebrating successes, individuals can develop a habit of punctuality that will lead to personal and professional success.

Ethics are the moral principles that govern our behavior and decision-making. In essence, they guide us on what is right and what is wrong. Living an ethical life is important to succeed in various aspects of our lives, including personal, professional, and social life.

First and foremost, being ethical in personal life means being true to oneself and others. It means maintaining integrity, honesty, and transparency in all our dealings with people. It also means respecting others and treating them with dignity, empathy, and compassion. When we are ethical in our personal lives, we build strong relationships based on trust, mutual respect, and shared values. This leads to happiness, contentment, and a sense of fulfillment in life.

Moreover, ethics play a vital role in professional life. It is the foundation for a successful career. Employers, customers, and colleagues expect professionals to uphold ethical standards of behavior, such as honesty, integrity, respect, and accountability. By following these standards, professionals can earn trust, build credibility, and enhance their reputation. They can also foster a positive work environment that promotes teamwork, innovation, and productivity.

Being ethical in professional life also helps in making sound business decisions. When ethical principles guide business practices, companies can avoid unethical practices such as bribery, fraud, or discrimination. Ethical practices also ensure that companies operate within the legal framework, and they adhere to industry standards and regulations. As a result, companies can avoid legal troubles, financial loss, and damage to their reputation.

Moreover, ethics are also important in social life. Being ethical means being responsible and contributing positively to society. It means respecting diversity, human rights, and the environment. When we are ethical in social life, we can create a better world for ourselves and future generations. We can also inspire others to follow ethical principles and make a difference in the world.

In addition to personal, professional, and social benefits, ethics have long-term benefits as well. Ethical values, such as honesty, integrity, and accountability, help individuals build character and become better persons. They also enhance self-awareness, self-esteem, and self-confidence. Moreover, ethical values create a sense of purpose and meaning in life, which leads to personal growth and development.

In contrast, unethical behavior can have severe consequences for individuals, organizations, and society. It can lead to loss of trust, reputation damage, legal troubles, financial loss, and social stigma. Unethical behavior can also create a toxic work environment, disrupt social harmony, and damage the environment. In extreme cases, unethical behavior can cause irreparable harm to individuals and society.

To stay ethical in life, one needs to cultivate certain habits and values. The first step is to be self-aware and reflective. This means examining our values, beliefs, and behavior patterns and identifying areas that need improvement. It also means being honest with ourselves and acknowledging our mistakes and weaknesses.

The second step is to practice ethical principles consistently. This means upholding honesty, integrity, respect, and accountability in all our dealings with people. It also means avoiding unethical practices such as lying, cheating, and stealing. It also means standing up for ethical values, even in the face of adversity.

The third step is to lead by example. This means being a role model for others by embodying ethical values in our behavior and decision-making. It also means inspiring and encouraging others to follow ethical principles.

Living an ethical life is essential to succeed in various aspects of our lives. Ethical values, such as honesty, integrity, respect, and accountability, form the foundation for personal, professional, and social success. They help individuals build strong relationships, earn trust, enhance their reputation, and make a positive impact on society. Ethical principles also lead to personal growth, development, and fulfillment. Therefore, it is crucial to cultivate

Martin Luther King Jr. was an American Baptist minister and civil rights activist who is widely recognized as one of the most influential leaders of the civil rights movement in the United States. His ethical principles were central to his work and continue to inspire people around the world today.

One of the most famous examples of King's ethical leadership is his commitment to nonviolence. King believed that nonviolent resistance was not only the most effective means of achieving change, but also the most moral. He saw violence as a cycle of hate that only perpetuated suffering and injustice, and he believed that true justice could only be achieved through peaceful means.

King's commitment to nonviolence was put to the test on numerous occasions, including during the Montgomery Bus Boycott in 1955 and the Birmingham Campaign in 1963. Despite facing violent opposition and enduring personal threats, King remained steadfast in his commitment to nonviolence and encouraged his followers to do the same. His leadership helped to create a movement that was not only effective, but also morally just.

Another example of King's ethical principles was his unwavering commitment to equality and justice for all people, regardless of race or background. He believed that every person was created equal and should be treated with respect and dignity. He fought against discrimination, segregation, and poverty, and he advocated for policies that would promote greater equality and opportunity for all.

King's commitment to justice and equality was demonstrated in many of his famous speeches and writings, including his "I Have a Dream" speech and his "Letter from Birmingham Jail." He inspired millions of people to work towards a more just and equitable society, and his legacy continues to inspire generations of activists and leaders around the world.

Martin Luther King Jr. was a powerful leader and advocate for justice and equality who exemplified ethical behavior throughout his life. His commitment to nonviolence, his dedication to equality and justice, and his unwavering principles continue to inspire people around the world today. His life and work remind us of the importance of standing up for what is right, even in the face of adversity, and of working towards a more just and equitable world for all.

Ethics refer to the principles and values that govern the behavior of individuals and organizations. These principles include honesty, integrity, accountability, respect for others, and responsibility. Ethics are essential in every aspect of our lives, including personal, professional, and societal. In this essay, we will explore why ethics are important in life, career, and success.

Firstly, ethics are important in our personal lives because they help us make responsible and informed decisions. Ethical principles guide our behavior and help us distinguish right from wrong. When we act ethically, we demonstrate a commitment to our values and principles. This not only leads to a sense of personal satisfaction and fulfillment, but also helps us build stronger relationships with others. Ethical behavior helps to establish trust, respect, and credibility, which are crucial for building meaningful and lasting relationships.

In addition to personal relationships, ethics are also essential for success in a career. Ethical behavior in the workplace is crucial for building trust and credibility with colleagues, clients, and customers. When employees and organizations act ethically, they demonstrate a commitment to doing the right thing, even when it may be difficult or unpopular. This can lead to increased trust and loyalty from customers, improved relationships with colleagues, and greater success in business.

Ethics are also important in the long-term success of a career. Individuals who act ethically and with integrity are more likely to be trusted and respected by others, and are therefore more likely to be promoted to positions of greater responsibility and influence. Ethics can also help to establish a positive reputation, which can lead to greater opportunities for success in the future.

Furthermore, ethics are essential for success in society as a whole. Society functions best when individuals and organizations act in accordance with ethical principles. Ethical behavior helps to build a sense of community and cooperation, and can lead to greater social and economic stability. Ethical behavior is also essential for addressing some of the world's most pressing problems, such as poverty, inequality, and environmental degradation. By acting ethically and responsibly, individuals and organizations can contribute to positive social change and help build a better future for all.

In addition to the benefits of ethical behavior, there are also negative consequences associated with unethical behavior. Unethical behavior can lead to legal and financial penalties, damage to reputation and trust, and harm to others. For example, unethical business practices can lead to lawsuits, loss of customers, and damage to brand reputation. Unethical behavior in personal relationships can lead to broken trust, damaged relationships, and emotional harm. Unethical behavior in society can lead to social and economic instability, and can perpetuate inequalities and injustices.

In conclusion, ethics are important in every aspect of our lives, including personal, professional, and societal. Ethical behavior helps us make responsible and informed decisions, builds trust and credibility with others, and contributes to positive social change. Ethics are essential for success in a career, as ethical behavior can lead to increased trust and credibility, greater opportunities for promotion, and a positive reputation. Finally, ethics are crucial for success in society, as ethical behavior can help to build a sense of community and cooperation, and contribute to positive social change. In contrast, unethical behavior can lead to negative consequences such as legal and financial penalties, damaged relationships and reputation, and harm to others. Therefore, it is essential for individuals and organizations to act ethically and with integrity in order to achieve personal and professional success, and to contribute to a more just and equitable society.

Practicing ethics is essential for success in personal and professional life. Here are some ways beginners can start practicing ethics:

1. Understand and define your values: Begin by reflecting on what you believe in, what is important to you, and

what kind of person you want to be. This can help you define your values and establish a foundation for ethical decision-making.

2. Act with integrity: Integrity means being honest and truthful in your actions and decisions. Always do what you say you will do, keep your promises, and be truthful in all your interactions with others.

3. Respect others: Treat others with dignity and respect, regardless of their background, status, or beliefs. Listen actively, avoid making assumptions, and practice empathy to understand others' perspectives.

4. Take responsibility for your actions: Be accountable for your decisions and actions, and admit to your mistakes. This helps to build trust and credibility with others.

5. Avoid conflicts of interest: Identify and avoid situations where your personal interest's conflict with your professional or ethical obligations. This can help you avoid unethical behavior and maintain your integrity.

6. Seek guidance: When faced with difficult ethical decisions, seek advice and guidance from trusted mentors, colleagues, or professionals. This can help you make informed decisions and avoid making mistakes.

7. Practice ethical decision-making: When faced with an ethical dilemma, take the time to reflect on your values, consider the consequences of your actions, and consult with others if necessary. This can help you make ethical decisions that align with your values and principles.

By practicing ethics, you can build trust and credibility with others, establish a positive reputation, and contribute to positive social change. Starting with small steps and developing a habit of ethical behavior can lead to long-term success and personal fulfillment.

ᐅᐅᐅ

Chapter Summary:

In this chapter, we delved into the significance of punctuality and ethics in different aspects of life, discovering their profound impact on our personal and professional spheres. Punctuality, as we learned, extends beyond simply arriving on time. It serves as a reflection of our commitment, reliability, and respect for others. By honoring our obligations and valuing punctuality, we not only demonstrate professionalism but also enhance productivity and foster trust in our relationships.

Ethics, on the other hand, emerged as a fundamental compass guiding our moral decision-making. We explored the importance of ethical principles in both personal and professional contexts, recognizing their role in establishing fairness, integrity, and accountability. Upholding ethics ensures that our actions align with our values, contributing to a just and harmonious society.

Moreover, we discussed how ethical decision-making encompasses various aspects, such as considering the potential consequences of our actions, respecting the rights and well-being of others, and adhering to principles of honesty and transparency. By integrating ethics into our daily lives, we not only make choices that benefit ourselves but also contribute to the greater good.

Throughout the chapter, we examined real-life examples and case studies that highlighted the profound impact of punctuality and ethics. We discovered that individuals and organizations known for their punctuality and ethical practices tend to enjoy stronger relationships, increased trust, and improved reputation.

In conclusion, punctuality and ethics serve as guiding principles that shape our behavior and interactions. By valuing punctuality, we demonstrate respect and reliability, while ethics provide the foundation for moral decision-making. Incorporating these principles into our lives enriches our personal and professional experiences, contributing to a more conscientious and harmonious society.

Activity:

The objective of this activity is to encourage readers to reflect on their punctuality and ethics and identify actionable steps they can take to improve these qualities on a daily basis, ultimately fostering personal and professional success.

1. *Self-Reflection: Take a moment to reflect on your current level of punctuality and ethics. Consider instances where you might have fallen short or situations where you have excelled. Reflect on the impact these qualities have on your relationships, productivity, and reputation.*
2. *Identify Areas for Improvement: Identify specific areas where you believe you can improve your punctuality and ethics. It could be arriving on time for meetings, meeting deadlines, practicing honesty in all interactions, or any other relevant aspect. Write down these areas as actionable goals.*
3. *Create an Action Plan: Develop an action plan that outlines steps you can take to enhance your punctuality and ethics. Break down each goal into smaller, manageable tasks. For example, if your goal is to improve punctuality, your action*

plan could include setting reminders, allocating buffer time for unforeseen circumstances, and prioritizing punctuality in your daily schedule.

4. *Seek Accountability: Share your action plan with a trusted friend, colleague, or mentor who can provide support and hold you accountable. Discuss your goals and ask for their feedback and suggestions. Regularly update them on your progress and seek guidance whenever needed.*

5. *Practice Mindfulness: Cultivate mindfulness in your daily activities to enhance your punctuality and ethics. Be present in the moment, consciously aware of your commitments and the impact of your actions. Consider the ethical implications of your decisions and strive to align your behavior with your values.*

6. *Reflect and Learn: Regularly reflect on your progress and evaluate the impact of your efforts. Consider the positive changes you have experienced and the challenges you have faced. Learn from both successes and setbacks, adjusting your action plan as necessary.*

7. *Share Experiences: Engage in discussions with peers, colleagues, or online communities about your journey towards improving punctuality and ethics. Share your experiences, insights, and lessons learned. Learn from others' experiences and exchange valuable tips and strategies.*

8. *Celebrate Milestones: Celebrate your achievements and milestones along the way. Recognize the progress you have made in enhancing your punctuality and ethics. Reward yourself for your commitment and dedication, reinforcing positive habits.*

Remember, improving punctuality and ethics is an ongoing journey that requires consistent effort and self-reflection. By actively incorporating these qualities into your daily life, you can create a positive impact not only on yourself but also on those around you, fostering success in various aspects of your personal and professional life.

❧❧❧

NINE

GRABBING OPPORTUNITIES: THE PATH TO SUCCESS

"Opportunity is missed by most people because it is dressed in overalls and looks like work." - Les Brown

Opportunities are all around us, waiting to be seized. However, it is important to note that not all opportunities are created equal, and that we should be discerning in our pursuit of them. The first step in identifying opportunities is to have a clear understanding of what we want to achieve in life, whether it is personal or professional success. Once we have set our goals, we can then begin to look for opportunities that align with our values and principles.

It is important to remember that not all opportunities are ethical, and that we should never pursue opportunities that involve causing harm to others or society. Such opportunities may seem tempting in the short-term, but they will only lead to regret and ultimately harm our chances of long-term success. Instead, we should focus on finding opportunities that benefit ourselves and those around us, without causing harm or undermining the well-being of others.

Moreover, opportunities should not be pursued at the expense of our values or principles. Our pursuit of success should be guided by a strong moral compass, and we should never compromise our ethics in order to achieve our goals. By staying true to our values, we can be confident that the opportunities we pursue will be aligned with our beliefs and will ultimately lead to a more fulfilling life.

It is also important to remember that opportunities are not always handed to us on a silver platter. We must be proactive in seeking out opportunities, and be willing to take risks and step out of our comfort zones. This may involve networking with others, learning new skills, or even starting our own ventures. By being proactive and constantly seeking out opportunities, we can ensure that we are always on the path to success.

At the same time, we must also be mindful of our own limitations and be willing to seek help and guidance when needed. No one can achieve success on their own, and we must be willing to collaborate with others and learn from their experiences. By working together and supporting one another, we can create a culture of growth and opportunity that benefits us all.

We should never pursue opportunities that cause harm to others or undermine our values, and we should always stay true to our ethics and principles. By being proactive, seeking help when needed, and working together, we can create a world of opportunity that benefits us all.

Andrew Carnegie, born in Scotland in 1835, was one of the most successful and influential industrialists of the 19th century. He built his fortune in the steel industry, but his rise to success was not without challenges and setbacks. Carnegie's story is one of seizing opportunities and taking risks to build a great business empire.

Carnegie started his career as a telegraph messenger in Pittsburgh, Pennsylvania, and worked his way up to become a telegraph operator and later a superintendent for the Pennsylvania Railroad Company. He recognized the potential of the growing steel industry and invested in the production of steel, eventually becoming the largest steel manufacturer in the United States and one of the wealthiest men of his time.

Here are some of the ways that Andrew Carnegie grabbed opportunities and built his business empire:

1. Recognizing the potential of new technologies: Carnegie was an early adopter of new technologies in the steel industry, including the Bessemer process, which made steel production more efficient and cost-effective.

2. Investing in infrastructure: Carnegie understood the importance of investing in infrastructure, including railroads, to transport steel products to markets around the world.

3. Focusing on cost-cutting measures: Carnegie was known for his focus on cost-cutting measures to increase efficiency and profitability. He implemented new

technologies and production methods that reduced the cost of steel production and enabled him to offer his products at competitive prices.

4. Expanding his business: Carnegie was not content to rest on his laurels and continued to expand his business through mergers and acquisitions. He acquired several other steel companies, including the Carnegie Steel Company, which he eventually sold to J.P. Morgan for $480 million in 1901.

Andrew Carnegie's story is a testament to the power of seizing opportunities and taking risks to build a great business empire. He recognized the potential of new technologies, invested in infrastructure, focused on cost-cutting measures, expanded his business through mergers and acquisitions, and used his wealth to fund philanthropic projects. His legacy continues to inspire entrepreneurs and business leaders around the world.

Grabbing opportunities is an essential part of achieving success in both personal and professional life. It requires a combination of a positive mindset, the willingness to take risks, and the ability to identify and capitalize on opportunities that come your way. One of the most critical aspects of grabbing opportunities is being prepared for them. By developing a strong foundation of skills, knowledge, and experience, you can position yourself to take advantage of opportunities as they arise.

To illustrate this point, consider the example of Amazon. In 1994, Jeff Bezos founded Amazon as an online bookstore. From the beginning, Bezos recognized the potential of the internet to transform the retail industry. He saw an opportunity to create a new kind of bookstore, one that was not limited by the physical constraints of a traditional brick-and-mortar store.

However, to capitalize on this opportunity, Bezos had to be prepared. He had to develop the necessary technological infrastructure to create an online store that could handle the demands of millions of customers. He had to build a team of employees who could help him execute his vision. And he had to be willing to take risks, investing large sums of money in the company even when it was not yet profitable.

Despite the challenges and risks, Bezos's vision paid off. Today, Amazon is one of the largest and most successful companies in the world, selling everything from books to electronics to groceries. By recognizing an opportunity, being prepared for it, and taking calculated risks, Bezos was able to turn a small online bookstore into a global behemoth.

So, what can we learn from Amazon's success story? The first lesson is to always be on the lookout for opportunities. Opportunities can come from many sources, including changes in technology, shifts in the market, and new social or cultural trends. The key is to be open-minded and curious, always seeking out new information and perspectives.

The second lesson is to be prepared for those opportunities when they arise. This means developing a strong foundation of skills and knowledge, building a network of supportive colleagues and mentors, and being willing to take risks. It also means having a clear sense of your values and goals, so that you can make informed decisions about which opportunities to pursue.

Finally, it's essential to be adaptable and flexible. Opportunities often come with unexpected challenges and setbacks, and the ability to adapt to changing circumstances is critical for success. By maintaining a growth mindset, staying focused on your goals, and being willing to pivot when necessary, you can increase your chances of turning an opportunity into a successful outcome.

Another great example of a company that seized an opportunity and became successful is Airbnb. Founded in 2008 by Brian Chesky, Joe Gebbia, and Nathan Blecharczyk, Airbnb began as a way for people to rent out air mattresses in their living rooms to attendees of a design conference in San Francisco. The idea was born out of necessity, as hotels in the area were fully booked and the founders needed to make rent money.

Seeing an opportunity to disrupt the hotel industry, Chesky, Gebbia, and Blecharczyk decided to turn this idea into a business. They launched Airbnb as a platform that allowed people to rent out their homes or apartments to travelers, providing an alternative to expensive hotels.

At first, the company struggled to gain traction, with only a few bookings in its first few months. However, the founders persisted and continued to improve the platform, adding new features and expanding to new markets. Eventually, Airbnb caught on, and the company grew rapidly, with listings in over 220 countries and a valuation of over $100 billion.

By capitalizing on an opportunity and providing a unique and affordable alternative to traditional lodging options, Airbnb was able to disrupt an entire industry and become a massive success. There are numerous such examples which we can learn from.

ৡৡৡ

One day, while working on a project, Brian and Harvey stumbled upon an idea for a new piece of software that would revolutionize the industry. They saw the opportunity and knew they had to seize it. They had been preparing for this moment for years, and they were ready to take the leap.

But it wasn't an easy decision. They would have to leave their comfortable jobs and steady income to start their own company. Brian and Harvey had always been proactive in their approach towards their careers. They were constantly on the lookout for opportunities that would allow them to achieve their dreams of starting their own software company.

They knew that success would only come if they were well prepared for any opportunity that came their way. So, they spent years honing their skills and building up their knowledge in the field of software development.

When the opportunity finally presented itself, they were ready. They had already convinced their respective families about the importance of their dream, and had saved enough money to sustain themselves for a year without a steady income. They had even started networking with potential clients and investors to ensure that they had the resources they needed to succeed.

But more importantly, Brian and Harvey had a strong belief in themselves and their abilities. They knew that their idea was unique and innovative, and that they had what it takes to make it a reality. They were confident in their skills and in their potential for success.

So, without hesitation, they took the leap and started their own company. They faced many challenges along the way, but their proactivity, preparedness, confidence, and belief in themselves kept them going. They were determined to make their dream a reality, and eventually, their hard work paid off. Their company became a huge success, and they were able to make a name for themselves in the industry.

Brian and Harvey's story is a testament to the power of being proactive, prepared, confident, and believing in oneself. It shows that with the right mindset and approach, anyone can seize the opportunities that come their way and achieve their dreams.

ϷϷϷ

Capitalizing on an opportunity effectively requires a strategic and focused approach. Firstly, it's important to conduct a thorough analysis of the opportunity at hand. This involves gathering as much information as possible about the opportunity, its potential risks and rewards, and any potential competitors. Once this analysis is complete, it's important to create a plan of action that outlines how you will leverage the opportunity to achieve your goals. This plan should include specific steps to be taken, timelines, and contingencies for potential roadblocks.

Another important aspect of capitalizing on an opportunity is to remain flexible and adaptable. Plans and strategies should be revised as new information is acquired and unexpected obstacles arise. In addition, it's important to remain open-minded and willing to pivot if necessary to capitalize on new opportunities that may present themselves.

Networking and collaboration are also key to effectively capitalizing on opportunities. Building relationships with others in your field or industry can help you stay informed about new developments and trends, and may lead to collaborative opportunities that can amplify your impact.

Finally, taking action and being decisive is crucial. It's important to move quickly and decisively when capitalizing on an opportunity, as delays or indecisiveness can cause you to miss out or lose momentum. However, it's also important to strike a balance between acting quickly and making thoughtful, informed decisions.

Overall, capitalizing on an opportunity effectively requires careful planning, flexibility, collaboration, and decisive action. By keeping these principles in mind, you can increase your chances of success and achieve your goals.

Are you waiting for your big break to come? Do you find yourself constantly daydreaming about that one perfect opportunity that will take you to the next level of success? If so, you're not alone. Many of us have dreams and aspirations that we hope will one day become a reality.

But here's the thing: opportunities for success rarely just fall into our laps. Instead, we have to actively seek them out and be willing to take risks in order to make them happen.

So how do we grab hold of those opportunities for success when they come our way?

Being prepared is not just a suggestion but a requirement to grab the opportunities that come our way. Opportunities can knock on our doors at any moment, so it's essential to be ready with the necessary skills, knowledge, and resources to take advantage of them.

I remember during my graduation days, most of my classmates and I had a common dream of traveling outside India for a project opportunity. One of my friends was fortunate enough to land a job in a reputed organization that provided him with such an opportunity. He was asked to fly to Singapore for an assignment, and it was a dream come true for him.

But unfortunately, he was unable to grab this opportunity, despite being so close, due to a lack of preparedness. He had never bothered to apply for a passport, which was a mandatory requirement to travel abroad. His unpreparedness cost him dearly, and he had to let go of the opportunity that he had worked so hard to achieve.

From this experience, I learned that opportunity favors the prepared mind. Being prepared is not just about having the right skills or knowledge; it's also about being mentally and physically ready to take on any challenge that comes your way.

So, if you want to make the most out of any opportunity, always be prepared. Keep your skills up-to-date, learn new things, network, and be ready to take calculated risks. Because you never know when the next big opportunity might knock on your door, and you want to be ready to open it.

When it comes to opportunities, it's crucial to take initiative and be proactive. I learned this firsthand during my early days as an entrepreneur, where I co-founded an edtech company. We were invited by a multinational corporation to participate in a day-long webinar aimed at establishing their products in the educational market. During a tea break, my co-founder and I saw a chance to connect with the director of the company and offered to address their pain points by becoming a partner and providing the necessary training. The next day, we were thrilled to become a partner with one of the most well-known MNCs in the field, assisting them in positioning their products in the educational vertical. This experience taught me that by being alert and seizing opportunities, we can achieve great success in our endeavors.

Sometimes opportunities for success may not look like what we initially envisioned. Be open to new ideas and be willing to adapt your plans as needed. Embrace change and be flexible in your approach to achieving your goals. Kodak was a dominant force in the photography industry for over a century, but the company's failure to seize on the opportunity to develop digital photography technology is often cited as one of the biggest missed opportunities in business history.

In the 1970s, Kodak's engineers developed the first digital camera, which was about the size of a toaster and had a resolution of 0.01 megapixels. However, Kodak's management was hesitant to embrace digital photography, as they believed it could potentially cannibalize their traditional film business.

Instead of focusing on digital photography, Kodak continued to invest in film technology and expanded their film product lines. The company also invested heavily in the development of new products, such as instant cameras and photo kiosks.

By the late 1990s, it became clear that digital photography was the future of the industry. Kodak's competitors, such as Canon and Nikon, were investing heavily in digital photography technology and were gaining market share. Kodak was slow to respond and continued to focus on film products.

In 2004, Kodak's new CEO, Antonio Perez, recognized the importance of digital photography and began a major restructuring effort to shift the company's focus to digital products. However, it was too little, too late. Kodak was facing intense competition from companies such as Sony and Canon, who had already established themselves as leaders in the digital photography market.

In 2012, Kodak filed for bankruptcy, citing the decline of the film industry and the company's failure to adapt to the digital age. Kodak's story is often cited as an example of the importance of innovation and the dangers of complacency. Despite being a dominant force in the industry for over a century, Kodak's failure to seize on the opportunity to develop digital photography technology ultimately led to its downfall.

Today, Kodak is still in business, but it is a shadow of its former self. The company now focuses on developing printing and packaging technologies, rather than photography. However, the legacy of Kodak's failure to embrace digital photography remains an important cautionary tale for businesses and entrepreneurs alike.

Another important aspect is one need to believe and have confidence in yourself and your abilities. Have confidence in your skills and your potential for success. Don't be afraid to take risks and put yourself out there – you never know what amazing opportunities may come your way.

When Musk founded SpaceX in 2002, many people thought he was crazy to try and create a private space company to compete with NASA. But Musk was confident in his abilities and had a clear vision for the future of space exploration. Despite facing numerous setbacks and failures along the way, Musk and his team continued to push forward, eventually achieving several historic milestones, such as the first privately funded spacecraft to reach orbit and the first commercial spacecraft to dock with the International Space Station.

Similarly, when Musk founded Tesla in 2003, he was met with skepticism from many in the auto industry who believed that electric cars would never catch on. But Musk believed in the potential of electric vehicles and set out to create a car that was not only environmentally friendly but also stylish and high-performing. Despite facing numerous production delays and financial challenges, Tesla has gone on to become a major player in the auto industry and has helped to accelerate the transition to electric vehicles around the world.

In both of these examples, Musk's belief in himself and his abilities, combined with his willingness to take risks and pursue his vision, led to incredible success and achievements that many thought were impossible.

To capitalize on opportunities, here are some key points to keep in mind:

1. Stay aware and alert: Keep your eyes and ears open for potential opportunities. This could involve staying up-to-date with the latest news and trends in your industry, attending networking events, or keeping in touch with contacts in your professional and personal networks.
2. Be prepared: Anticipate potential opportunities and prepare yourself to take advantage of them. This may involve updating your resume or portfolio, building up your savings, or acquiring new skills.
3. Be adaptable: Be open to change and willing to take risks. Don't be afraid to try new things or explore different paths to achieve your goals.
4. Develop skills: Stay current with the skills required in your industry and invest in your personal and professional development. This may involve taking courses, attending workshops, or seeking mentorship.
5. Build relationships: Develop strong relationships with colleagues, mentors, and other professionals in your industry. These connections can provide valuable insights, support, and opportunities for collaboration.
6. Take action: Don't wait for opportunities to come to you - take the initiative to create them. Be proactive in seeking

out new opportunities, and be prepared to take action when they arise.

7. Stay positive: Maintaining a positive attitude and mindset can help you stay motivated and focused on your goals, even in the face of challenges and setbacks.

ϷϷϷ

Chapter Summary:

In this chapter, we explored the importance of seizing opportunities for success. We emphasized that not all opportunities are created equal, and it is crucial to discern which ones align with our values and principles. We highlighted the significance of ethical decision-making, emphasizing that opportunities should never involve causing harm to others or society.

Furthermore, we discussed the need to stay true to our values and principles and not compromise our ethics in the pursuit of success. We acknowledged that opportunities may not always be readily available and that we must proactively seek them out, take risks, and step out of our comfort zones. We emphasized the importance of seeking help and guidance when needed and collaborating with others to create a culture of growth and opportunity.

To illustrate the concept of seizing opportunities, we presented the stories of Andrew Carnegie, Jeff Bezos, and the founders of Airbnb. We showcased how Carnegie recognized the potential of new technologies, invested in infrastructure, focused on cost-cutting measures, and expanded his business through mergers and acquisitions. We demonstrated how Bezos capitalized on the opportunity presented by the internet and built Amazon into a global powerhouse. We also highlighted how the founders of Airbnb identified a gap in the market and created a disruptive alternative to traditional lodging options.

Throughout the chapter, we underscored the need for preparation, proactive action, adaptability, and belief in oneself. We shared examples of missed opportunities, such as Kodak's failure to embrace digital photography, to emphasize the dangers of complacency and the importance of innovation. Finally, we concluded by encouraging readers to have confidence in their abilities and be willing to take risks, as amazing opportunities can arise when least expected.

Overall, the chapter emphasized that seizing opportunities requires a combination of strategic planning, flexibility, collaboration, decisive action, and belief in oneself. By applying these principles, individuals can increase their chances of success and achieve their goals.

Activity:

To develop the mindset and skills necessary to identify and seize opportunities for personal and professional success.

1. *Reflect on your goals: Take a few moments to think about your short-term and long-term goals. Consider your aspirations, dreams, and what you hope to achieve in different areas of your life, such as career, relationships, health, or personal development. Write them down in detail.*
2. *Brainstorm potential opportunities: Grab a pen and paper or open a document on your computer. Make a list of potential opportunities that align with your goals. Think about the*

current trends, technologies, or social changes that may create opportunities in your desired field. Don't limit yourself—let your imagination run wild and jot down as many ideas as you can.

3. *Evaluate the opportunities: Review the list of potential opportunities you brainstormed and evaluate each one based on the following criteria:*

4. *Relevance: Assess how closely each opportunity aligns with your goals and values. Consider how pursuing the opportunity could contribute to your overall success and fulfillment.*

5. *Feasibility: Analyze the feasibility of each opportunity. Take into account your skills, resources, and current circumstances. Can you realistically pursue and capitalize on this opportunity given your current situation?*

6. *Potential risks and rewards: Consider the potential risks and rewards associated with each opportunity. Evaluate the potential benefits that could arise from seizing the opportunity, as well as any potential challenges or drawbacks that may come along with it.*

7. *Select the most promising opportunities: Based on your evaluations, identify the two or three most promising opportunities that have the highest potential to move you closer to your goals.*

8. *Create an action plan: For each selected opportunity, create a detailed action plan that outlines the steps you need to take to seize the opportunity. Break down the plan into smaller, actionable tasks with specific deadlines. Consider the resources, skills, and support you may need to acquire along the way.*

9. *Take immediate action: Start taking action on your plans without delay. Begin with the tasks that can be accomplished quickly and build momentum from there.*

Embrace a proactive mindset and be open to adjusting your plans as you progress.

10. *Track your progress: Regularly review your progress and make adjustments to your action plans as needed. Stay committed and motivated, and celebrate even the smallest wins along the way.*

Remember, opportunity grabbing requires perseverance, adaptability, and a willingness to step out of your comfort zone. By engaging in this exercise and actively seeking out opportunities, you'll be better prepared to seize the right moments and maximize your chances of success.

Best of luck on your journey of opportunity grabbing!

ᗡᗡᗡ

TEN

PERSISTENCE: NEVER GIVING UP

"Our greatest weakness lies in giving up. The most certain way to succeed is always to try just one more time." - Thomas Edison

ᐅᐅᐅ

Persistence is an essential trait for success, and it is the key ingredient that differentiates successful individuals from unsuccessful ones. Persistence is the ability to continue pursuing a goal or objective despite encountering obstacles, setbacks, and failures. It is the determination to keep pushing forward despite the challenges and roadblocks that might stand in the way.

The human mind is a complex and powerful tool that can be harnessed to achieve great things. One of the key traits that can help individuals achieve success is persistence. The ability to stay committed to a goal or task in the face of challenges and setbacks is a powerful attribute that can lead to great accomplishments.

Persistence is a characteristic that is observed across the animal kingdom, from insects to primates. It is a behavior that involves continuing to pursue a goal despite challenges or setbacks. In humans, persistence has been linked to success in many areas of life, including education, career, and personal relationships. In recent years, researchers have begun to explore the neurological and physiological mechanisms that underlie persistence in the human brain, as well as in other animals.

The human brain is a complex organ that is still not fully understood by scientists. However, studies have shown that certain areas of the brain are associated with persistence. For example, the prefrontal cortex, which is located in the front of the brain, has been linked to the ability to set goals and work towards them. In addition, the anterior cingulate cortex, which is located deeper in the brain, has been linked to the ability to monitor and regulate behavior, which is important for staying on task and avoiding distractions.

Other studies have found that the neurotransmitter dopamine may play a role in persistence. Dopamine is a chemical that is released in the brain in response to rewards, and it has been shown to be involved in motivation and goal-directed behavior. When we achieve a goal or experience a reward, dopamine is released, which reinforces the behavior and encourages us to continue pursuing the goal.

Another animal that is often cited as an example of persistence is the honeybee. Honeybees are known for their ability to navigate long distances and find their way back to their hive, even in the face of challenges such as wind, rain, and changing landscapes. Researchers have found that honeybees use a combination of visual landmarks and odor cues to navigate, and that they are able to adapt to changes in their environment by updating their mental map of the area.

In addition to these examples from the animal kingdom, there are many examples of human persistence that have been studied by researchers. For example, a study published in the Journal of Educational Psychology found that students who were more persistent in their academic pursuits were more likely to achieve their goals and perform well in school. The study also found that students who had a growth mindset, or a belief that intelligence and ability can be developed through effort, were more likely to be persistent than those who had a fixed mindset.

Another study, published in the journal Frontiers in Psychology, found that persistence was associated with better mental health outcomes in young adults. The study found that young adults who were more persistent in pursuing their goals were less likely to experience symptoms of depression and anxiety, and were more likely to report higher levels of life satisfaction.

Overall, persistence is a characteristic that is observed across the animal kingdom, and is essential for success in many areas of life. In humans, persistence is associated with specific areas of the brain, and is linked to the neurotransmitter dopamine. Animals such as honeybees are known for their persistence, and there are many examples of human persistence that have been studied by researchers. As our understanding of the brain and behavior continues to evolve, it is likely that we will learn even more about the mechanisms that underlie persistence, and the ways in which we can cultivate this important characteristic in ourselves and others.

However, persistence is not always easy to maintain. The human mind is naturally inclined to seek out comfort and avoid pain, and the challenges and obstacles that come with pursuing a goal can sometimes feel overwhelming. This is where the power of the mind comes into play.

By training the mind to focus on the positive aspects of a goal, and to stay motivated and committed in the face of adversity, individuals can cultivate a sense of inner strength and resilience that can help them overcome even the most difficult challenges. This may involve techniques such as visualization, positive self-talk, and mindfulness, which can help individuals stay centered and focused even in the midst of chaos.

Another key aspect of persistence is the ability to learn from failure and setbacks. Rather than giving up when faced with an obstacle, persistent individuals use these experiences as opportunities for growth and learning. They analyze what went wrong, make adjustments as needed, and try again with renewed determination and focus.

Ultimately, the key to harnessing the power of the mind and developing a sense of persistence is to cultivate a positive mindset and a strong sense of purpose. By staying focused on your goals, maintaining a positive attitude, and being willing to learn and grow along the way, you can develop a powerful sense of inner strength and resilience that can help you achieve great things in all areas of your life.

Persistence is critical for success because it enables individuals to stay focused and committed to their goals even when the going gets tough. It is a quality that helps people to stay motivated and dedicated to their objectives, even in the face of adversity. When people encounter challenges or setbacks, persistence helps them to overcome those obstacles and find creative solutions to the problems they encounter.

One of the main reasons that persistence is so crucial for success is that success often requires time and effort. Most significant achievements do not happen overnight, and they require hard work, dedication, and perseverance to accomplish. Whether it is building a successful business, achieving a personal goal, or pursuing a career, success often requires sustained effort and commitment over an extended period.

For example, think about a person who wants to become a professional athlete. This individual will need to practice and train regularly, even when they do not feel like it. They will need to push themselves to their limits, both physically and mentally, and be persistent in their pursuit of excellence. They will need to endure setbacks, injuries, and failures along the way, but if they stay persistent, they can achieve their goal of becoming a successful athlete.

Similarly, in business, persistence is essential for success. Many successful entrepreneurs have had to overcome significant challenges and obstacles to build successful companies. They have had to persist through tough economic times, intense competition, and other setbacks to achieve their goals. But by remaining persistent, they were able to find ways to overcome those obstacles and create successful businesses.

Persistence is a key trait that can help individuals achieve success in their personal and professional lives. This is especially true in sales, where the ability to be persistent can often make the difference between closing a deal or losing a customer.

Have you ever come across a salesperson who was persistent in their efforts to sell you a product or idea? How did you respond? Perhaps you felt annoyed at first, but then you recognized their honest efforts and rewarded them with your purchase. This experience can be a valuable lesson in the power of persistence.

When it comes to being persistent, there are a few key factors that can make a difference in how others respond to your efforts. First and foremost, it's important to be genuine and sincere in your approach. People can often sense when someone is being insincere or pushy, and this can quickly turn them off.

Another important factor is to be respectful of others' time and boundaries. Persistence does not mean being obnoxious or overbearing - it means being committed to your goals while also being mindful of the needs and preferences of others.

Additionally, persistence often requires a willingness to take risks and try new things. This may involve stepping outside of your comfort zone, making mistakes, and learning from them. However, with persistence comes the potential for reward, and the ability to achieve your goals and fulfill your dreams.

If you are looking to improve your own persistence, it can be helpful to set specific goals and develop a plan of action for achieving them. This may involve breaking your goals down into smaller, more manageable steps, and tracking your progress along the way. It can also be helpful to seek out feedback from others, whether it's from a mentor, coach, or trusted friend.

Another reason why persistence is critical for success is that it helps people develop the necessary skills and expertise to achieve their goals. When people persist in their pursuits, they gain valuable experience and knowledge that can help them overcome future challenges and obstacles. By staying persistent, individuals can develop a deep understanding of their field, their market, and their customers, which can help them make better decisions and achieve their goals more effectively.

For instance, think about a person who wants to become a successful writer. This individual will need to write regularly, even when they do not feel inspired. They will need to read extensively, study their craft, and seek feedback from others to improve their skills. Over time, this persistence will enable them to become a better writer, develop their unique voice and style, and eventually achieve success in their field.

Finally, persistence is essential for success because it helps people develop resilience and mental toughness. When individuals persist in their pursuits, they learn how to overcome adversity, deal with failure, and stay focused on their goals despite setbacks. This resilience and mental toughness are critical qualities for success in any field, as they help people to maintain their confidence, stay motivated, and keep moving forward despite challenges.

For example, think about a person who wants to start their own business. This individual will need to deal with a variety of challenges, such as raising capital, finding customers, and building a team. They will encounter setbacks and failures along the way, but by staying persistent, they can develop the resilience and mental toughness necessary to keep pushing forward, even when the going gets tough.

In conclusion, persistence is a critical quality for success in any field. It enables individuals to stay focused and committed to their goals, develop the skills and expertise necessary to achieve those goals, and develop the resilience and mental toughness required to overcome challenges and setbacks. By staying persistent, individuals can achieve their goals and reach their full potential, even in the face of adversity.

One of the most famous examples of persistence in history is the story of the American frontiersman and mountain man, Hugh Glass. Glass was a trapper and explorer in the early 1800s, and he is perhaps best known for his incredible survival story after being mauled by a grizzly bear.

In 1823, Glass was part of a group of trappers exploring the Upper Missouri River when he was attacked by a grizzly bear. The bear severely injured Glass, leaving him with a broken leg, deep cuts, and other injuries. Glass's companions thought he would surely die from his injuries and left him behind, taking his equipment and supplies with them.

Despite his injuries, Glass refused to give up. He set his own broken leg, wrapped himself in a bear hide, and began crawling and dragging himself across the prairie toward the nearest trading post, which was over 200 miles away. Glass was determined to survive and return to civilization, no matter what it took.

For six weeks, Glass crawled and dragged himself across the harsh terrain, through freezing temperatures and with little food or water. He survived by eating berries and roots and catching small animals along the way. Eventually, he made it to the Cheyenne River, where he fashioned a makeshift raft and floated the remaining miles to Fort Kiowa, a trading post where he could receive medical attention.

Glass's incredible story of survival has become the stuff of legend, and it is a testament to his incredible persistence and determination. Despite being severely injured and left for dead, he refused to give up and instead persevered through incredible hardship and adversity to achieve his goal of returning to civilization.

In the end, Glass's persistence paid off. He survived his injuries and went on to become a legendary figure in the American West, known for his incredible survival skills and his unwavering determination in the face of adversity. His story is a powerful reminder that persistence and determination can help us overcome even the most difficult challenges and achieve our goals, no matter how daunting they may seem.

One of the most inspiring stories of persistence in India is that of a man named Dashrath Manjhi, also known as the "Mountain Man". Manjhi was a poor laborer from a remote village in Bihar, a state in northern India. In 1959, his wife, Falguni Devi, died from a lack of medical attention, as the nearest hospital was located on the other side of a large mountain range.

Manjhi was devastated by his wife's death and determined to find a way to make sure that no one else in his village would suffer the same fate. He decided to take matters into his own hands and began chiseling away at the mountain with just a hammer and chisel, determined to create a path through the mountain so that people could travel to the hospital more easily.

For the next 22 years, Manjhi worked tirelessly, day and night, chiseling away at the mountain, one rock at a time. He faced numerous obstacles and setbacks along the way, including ridicule from his fellow villagers, who thought he was insane for taking on such a monumental task.

Despite these challenges, Manjhi refused to give up. He continued to chip away at the mountain, creating a path that was 360 feet long, 25 feet deep, and 30 feet wide. His perseverance and hard work paid off when the path was finally completed in 1982, reducing the distance to the nearest hospital from 55 kilometers to just one kilometer.

Manjhi's incredible feat of persistence and determination made him a hero in his village and throughout India. He passed away in 2007, but his legacy lives on as a symbol of the power of persistence and determination.

Manjhi's story is a testament to the human spirit and the power of persistence. Despite facing seemingly insurmountable obstacles, he refused to give up and instead dedicated his life to creating a better future for his village. His example serves as an inspiration to all of us, reminding us that with hard work and determination, anything is possible.

Michael Jordan is a prime example of how persistence and determination can lead to great success. Jordan is widely regarded as one of the greatest basketball players of all time, but his path to success was not without its challenges.

Jordan was initially cut from his high school basketball team, a setback that could have easily deterred him from pursuing a career in the sport. However, Jordan refused to give up on his dream and instead channeled his disappointment into a fierce determination to improve his skills and prove his worth as a basketball player.

This persistence paid off, as Jordan went on to play for the University of North Carolina and was eventually drafted by the Chicago Bulls in 1984. Over the course of his career, Jordan won six NBA championships, five MVP awards, and numerous other accolades.

But Jordan's success was not simply a result of his natural talent. It was also a product of his tireless work ethic and dedication to the sport. Jordan was known for his grueling training regimen, which included hours of practice and conditioning drills each day. He was also known for his mental toughness and ability to stay focused and motivated in the face of challenges and setbacks.

One of Jordan's most famous examples of persistence came during the 1995-1996 NBA season, when he led the Chicago Bulls to a record-breaking 72-10 regular season record. Despite facing numerous obstacles throughout the season, including injuries and personal struggles, Jordan refused to give up and instead redoubled his efforts to lead his team to victory.

Jordan's persistence and dedication to the sport of basketball have inspired countless individuals around the world to pursue their own dreams and goals with the same level of determination and commitment. By embodying these qualities in his own life and career, Jordan has left a lasting legacy not just as a basketball player, but as a role model for anyone who seeks to achieve greatness through hard work, persistence, and determination.

TOMS is a prime example of a company that has made a conscious effort to prioritize social impact over profit margins. Since its inception, the company has been focused on the idea of "One for One" - for every product sold, TOMS donates a product or service to a person in need. TOMS' original product was shoes, but the company has since expanded its "One for One" model to include eyewear and coffee.

TOMS' commitment to social impact has not wavered, even as the company has grown and faced its share of challenges. In addition to its "One for One" giving programs, TOMS has launched various initiatives to support causes such as mental health and gun violence prevention.

One of the key factors in TOMS' persistence in its mission is the company's ability to effectively communicate its message and build a community of supporters. TOMS has created a strong brand identity around its social impact mission, which has resonated with consumers and inspired them to support the company's products and giving programs.

Furthermore, TOMS has been transparent about its giving programs and impact, regularly sharing updates and stories about the people who have been helped by the company's donations. This has helped to build trust with consumers and maintain the company's reputation as a socially responsible business.

TOMS' persistence in its commitment to social impact has also helped the company to differentiate itself in a crowded marketplace. By prioritizing social impact over profit margins, TOMS has attracted a loyal customer base who appreciate the company's values and mission.

Overall, TOMS serves as an inspiring example of how companies can use their resources and influence to make a positive impact on the world. By remaining persistent in their commitment to social impact and effectively communicating their message to consumers, companies like TOMS can create a better future for everyone.

Persistence is a trait that can make all the difference in achieving your goals and realizing your dreams. Whether it's in your personal life or in your career, developing persistence can help you overcome obstacles, stay focused on your objectives, and ultimately achieve success. Here are some tips for cultivating persistence in your life:

1. Set clear goals: Having clear goals can give you direction and motivation, which can help you stay focused and

persistent. Make sure your goals are specific, measurable, and achievable.

2. Break goals into small steps: Breaking down larger goals into smaller, more manageable tasks can help you avoid feeling overwhelmed and make it easier to stay on track. Celebrate small successes along the way to stay motivated.

3. Develop a growth mindset: A growth mindset means believing that you can improve and develop your skills and abilities over time. Embrace challenges as opportunities to learn and grow, rather than viewing them as obstacles.

4. Embrace failure: Failure is a natural part of the learning process, and it's important not to let setbacks discourage you. Instead, use failure as an opportunity to learn and improve.

5. Practice self-discipline: Self-discipline is the ability to make yourself do what needs to be done, even when you don't feel like it. Develop habits and routines that help you stay focused and productive.

6. Surround yourself with supportive people: Having supportive friends and family members can help you stay motivated and committed to your goals. Seek out people who encourage and inspire you.

7. Stay positive: A positive attitude can help you stay motivated and persistent, even when things get tough. Focus on the progress you've made and believe in your ability to achieve your goals.

ﭘﭘﭘ

After starting their own software company, Brian and Harvey faced several challenges. Despite their best efforts, one of their main investors suddenly pulled out, leaving them in a precarious financial situation. But Brian and Harvey refused to give up.

They were persistent in their pursuit of success, and they knew that giving up was not an option. They believed in themselves and their vision for the company, and they were confident that they could turn things around.

Despite the setback, Brian and Harvey were undaunted. They rolled up their sleeves and got to work, determined to convince other investors to believe in their company. They were proactive in their search, reaching out to potential investors and presenting their vision for the company in the most compelling way possible.

Their persistence eventually paid off. They were able to convince several new investors to come on board, and they received the funding they needed to continue growing their business. The company began to thrive, and Brian and Harvey became well-respected figures in the tech industry.

Brian and Harvey refused to let setbacks get in the way of their dreams, and they worked tirelessly to achieve their goals. Through their unwavering commitment to success, they were able to turn their dream into a reality.

ᚦᚦᚦ

Chapter Summary:

In this chapter, we explored the concept of persistence as a critical trait for success. We discussed how persistence involves staying committed to goals and objectives despite obstacles and setbacks. We examined the neurological and physiological mechanisms behind persistence in the human brain and explored examples of persistence in both the animal kingdom and human endeavors.

We learned that persistence requires cultivating a positive mindset, focusing on the positive aspects of a goal, and learning from failures and setbacks. We saw how persistence plays a crucial role in achieving success in various areas, such as education, career, and personal relationships. We also discussed the importance of time and effort in attaining significant accomplishments and how persistence helps individuals stay motivated and dedicated throughout the journey.

Furthermore, we highlighted the role of persistence in sales and emphasized the significance of being genuine, respectful, and mindful of others' needs in our pursuit of goals. We discussed the importance of taking risks, stepping out of comfort zones, and seeking feedback to foster personal growth and development.

Finally, we explored how persistence helps individuals gain valuable skills, expertise, and resilience that contribute to their success. By staying persistent, individuals can overcome challenges, develop a deep understanding of their field, and maintain mental toughness and resilience.

Activity:

1. *Set Clear and Specific Goals: Setting clear and specific goals provides a clear direction and purpose, making it easier to stay focused and motivated. Having a well-defined target helps you understand what you need to do to achieve it, allowing you to maintain persistence throughout the journey.*

2. *Break Goals into Manageable Steps:* Breaking goals into smaller, manageable steps provides a sense of progress and accomplishment along the way. Each step achieved reinforces your motivation to continue and builds momentum, fueling your persistence.

3. *Track Progress and Celebrate Milestones:* Tracking your progress allows you to see how far you've come and provides a sense of achievement. Celebrating milestones, no matter how small, boosts your confidence and reinforces your persistence by recognizing and acknowledging your progress.

4. *Cultivate a Positive Mindset:* A positive mindset enhances persistence by focusing on the positive aspects of your goals and progress. Positive self-talk and affirmations build belief in your ability to overcome challenges and keep going, even when faced with setbacks or difficulties.

5. *Learn from Setbacks and Failure:* Viewing setbacks and failure as opportunities for growth cultivates resilience and strengthens persistence. Analyzing what went wrong helps you learn valuable lessons, make necessary adjustments, and approach future challenges with greater determination and adaptability.

6. *Seek Feedback and Guidance:* Seeking feedback from mentors and trusted individuals provides fresh perspectives and insights. Their guidance helps you refine your approach, identify blind spots, and build new skills, boosting your confidence and reinforcing persistence.

7. *Embrace Resilience and Perseverance:* Embracing resilience and perseverance means staying committed to your goals despite obstacles or discouragement. It involves maintaining a long-term perspective, remembering your purpose, and using setbacks as stepping stones towards success.

8. *Practice Visualization and Mindfulness: Visualization techniques help you mentally rehearse success and reinforce your belief in achieving your goals. Mindfulness practices cultivate focus and resilience by keeping you present, aware of distractions, and grounded in the face of challenges or self-doubt.*

9. *Take Calculated Risks and Step Out of Comfort Zones: Taking calculated risks and stepping out of your comfort zone expands your abilities and cultivates adaptability. By embracing new experiences and challenges, you build resilience and discover new strengths, increasing your overall persistence.*

10. *Reflect and Review: Regular reflection and review of your progress help you celebrate achievements, recognize growth, and recalibrate as needed. This process keeps you aligned with your goals, provides clarity, and allows you to continually refine your approach, fostering long-term persistence.*

By implementing these strategies, you enhance your persistence by creating a supportive framework that reinforces your motivation, resilience, and adaptability. Clear goals, progress tracking, positive mindset, learning from setbacks, seeking guidance, and embracing resilience and mindfulness all work together to strengthen your persistence, empowering you to overcome challenges and achieve your desired success.

ppp

ELEVEN

WORK-LIFE BALANCE: FINDING HARMONY

We think, mistakenly, that success is the result of the amount of time we put in at work, instead of the quality of time we put in." - Arianna Huffington

Before the Industrial Revolution, work was largely based on agriculture and trade, and most people worked from home or within small, family-owned businesses. This meant that work hours were more flexible, allowing people to manage their time in a way that suited their personal needs. They could work at their own pace, take breaks when needed, and balance their work with other responsibilities, such as caring for children or elderly family members.

In these times, work was often closely tied to the community and family life. People would often work with their family members, and work and leisure activities were often integrated into the same spaces. There was no separation between the home and the workplace, and people had more control over their work environment and schedules. This allowed them to prioritize their personal needs and relationships, and have a more balanced and fulfilling life.

Moreover, people's relationship with work was different than today. Work was seen as a means of survival and a way to contribute to the community, rather than a source of wealth and status. This meant that people were less likely to sacrifice their personal lives for work, and work was not seen as the sole source of identity or purpose.

Overall, the pre-industrial work environment allowed for a greater degree of work-life balance, allowing people to prioritize their personal lives and responsibilities while still being productive members of their communities. However, with the rise of industrialization and the factory system, this balance was disrupted, leading to long working hours, rigid schedules, and a separation between work and personal life.

The Industrial Revolution began in the 18th century in Britain and quickly spread throughout Europe and North America. It was a time of significant technological advancements, including the development of machines and factories. However, the rise of the factory system and the need for round-the-clock production had a negative impact on work life balance. Workers were forced to work long hours, often in dangerous and unhealthy conditions. The focus was on maximizing production and profits, rather than the well-being of workers. This led to a high rate of workplace injuries and illnesses, including the infamous "black lung" disease in coal miners.

The negative impact of the Industrial Revolution on work life balance is still being felt today. Many industries still prioritize profits over the well-being of their employees. Long work hours, overtime, and irregular schedules are all common, leading to stress, burnout, and other negative health effects. According to a study conducted by the National Institute for Occupational Safety and Health, long work hours increase the risk of depression, anxiety, and sleep disorders. Furthermore, lack of work life balance can also lead to strained personal relationships, which can have further negative impacts on mental health and overall well-being.

Despite the negative side effects of the Industrial Revolution, many companies today still prioritize profits over employee well-being. The focus on productivity and efficiency has led to a culture of overworking, where employees are expected to work long hours and be available at all times. This has led to calls for a better work life balance, with some companies implementing policies such as flexible schedules, remote work, and unlimited vacation time. However, there is still a long way to go to ensure that all workers are able to achieve a healthy work life balance.

Our bodies and minds have evolved over millions of years to be in sync with the natural cycles of the Earth. Our circadian rhythm, which regulates our sleep-wake cycle, is closely tied to the natural cycle of light and dark. For most of human history, people lived and worked in harmony with these natural cycles. They woke up at sunrise and went to bed at sunset, and their work was usually done during daylight hours.

However, the Industrial Revolution and modern globalization have changed all that. With factories and offices operating 24/7 and people working across multiple time zones, the natural rhythms of the human body have been disrupted. This can lead to a host of health problems, both physical and mental.

Studies have shown that shift workers, who work outside of normal daylight hours, are more likely to suffer from sleep disorders, digestive problems, and cardiovascular disease. The disruption of the circadian rhythm can also lead to depression, anxiety, and other mental health issues.

Furthermore, our bodies and minds are designed to rest and recover after periods of activity. Without proper rest, we become fatigued and less productive, which can lead to even more stress and burnout. In fact, research has shown that chronic overwork and stress can lead to a host of health problems, including high blood pressure, heart disease, and stroke.

It is important to recognize that our bodies and minds are not designed to work around the clock. While it may be necessary to work outside of normal daylight hours in certain situations, it is important to balance that with proper rest and recovery. Taking breaks, getting enough sleep, and engaging in stress-reducing activities like exercise and meditation can all help to mitigate the negative effects of working outside of natural rhythms.

In short, it is important to remember that we are part of the natural world, and that our bodies and minds are designed to work in harmony with it. While modern technology and globalization have made it easier to work around the clock, it is important to prioritize work-life balance and take steps to mitigate the negative effects of working outside of natural rhythms.

Achieving a healthy work-life balance is crucial for career success and overall well-being. It's important to prioritize this habit from early career days, as it can have a profound impact on our lives and careers.

One of the key benefits of a healthy work-life balance is preventing burnout. When we neglect our personal lives and focus solely on work, we can quickly become exhausted, stressed, and overwhelmed. This can lead to burnout, which can have serious consequences for our health and well-being. By prioritizing a healthy work-life balance from the beginning, we can avoid burnout and maintain our energy and enthusiasm for our work.

Another benefit of a healthy work-life balance is increased productivity. When we take breaks, engage in non-work activities, and prioritize our personal lives, we are more likely to be productive when we are on the job. Studies have shown that employees who take breaks and engage in non-work activities are more creative and effective problem solvers. By making time for our personal lives, we can enhance our overall productivity and effectiveness.

A healthy work-life balance can also improve our relationships with others. When we prioritize our personal lives, we are able to connect more deeply with family and friends, and build stronger, more supportive relationships. This can provide a source of emotional and social support during challenging times, which can help us to be more resilient in the face of adversity.

Furthermore, a healthy work-life balance can help us avoid regrets later in life. Many people look back on their lives and regret not spending more time with family and friends, or not pursuing their hobbies and interests. By prioritizing a healthy work-life balance from early career days, we can avoid these regrets and ensure that we are living a full and satisfying life.

Finally, prioritizing a healthy work-life balance from early career days can set us up for long-term success. By developing habits and routines that prioritize our personal lives, we can avoid the trap of overworking and burning out, and instead build sustainable, fulfilling careers that align with our values and priorities. This can lead to greater job satisfaction, career advancement, and overall success.

Sheryl Sandberg is a prominent figure in the tech industry, known for her leadership roles at Google and Facebook. She is also an author, philanthropist, and advocate for gender equality in the workplace. Despite her busy schedule and demanding career, Sandberg is known for her commitment to maintaining a healthy work-life balance.

Sandberg's approach to work-life balance can be seen in her book, "Lean In: Women, Work, and the Will to Lead." In the book, she discusses the importance of prioritizing personal and family life, even while pursuing a demanding career. She encourages women to be assertive and intentional in their careers, but also to recognize the value of personal relationships and self-care.

Sandberg's commitment to work-life balance is evident in her daily routines and habits. She is known for leaving work at a reasonable hour to spend time with her family, and for taking vacations to recharge and reset. She also prioritizes exercise, meditation, and other forms of self-care to maintain her physical and mental health.

One example of Sandberg's commitment to work-life balance occurred in 2015, when her husband unexpectedly passed away. Despite the devastating loss, Sandberg took time off from work to focus on her family and her own well-being. She was open about her struggles with grief and her efforts to maintain a healthy work-life balance during this difficult time, and she received widespread support and admiration for her courage and resilience.

Sandberg's example has inspired many people to prioritize work-life balance in their own lives. Her message resonates with those who feel overwhelmed by the demands of their careers and personal lives, and who struggle to find a sense of balance and fulfillment. She demonstrates that it is possible to achieve success without sacrificing personal relationships, self-care, and other important aspects of life.

While it is true that we cannot change the entire industry, it is within our power to address the problem of work-life balance at our personal level. We can start by setting boundaries and being more mindful of our time. We can prioritize our personal life and make sure that work does not take over. We can also work towards building a culture of work-life balance within our teams and organizations. By leading by example and encouraging others to do the same, we can create a ripple effect that could ultimately lead to a change in the industry as a whole.

It is essential to understand that change starts from within. By making small changes in our own lives, we can inspire others to do the same. As individuals, we have the power to make a difference, and it is important to recognize that. It may take time to see the effects of our actions, but every step we take towards achieving work-life balance is a step in the right direction.

If you are in a leadership position, you have an even greater opportunity to influence change. By prioritizing work-life balance within your organization and making it a core value, you can create a positive work environment that supports the well-being of your employees. When employees feel valued and supported, they are more likely to be productive and engaged in their work.

In conclusion, while the problem of work-life balance may seem daunting, it is not impossible to address. By taking responsibility for our own work-life balance and encouraging others to do the same, we can make a positive impact on our own lives and the lives of those around us. Remember, change starts from within, and it is up to each one of us to make a difference.

Sandberg's work also highlights the broader importance of work-life balance in the tech industry and beyond. The tech industry is known for its intense work culture, with long hours and high pressure to succeed. This can lead to burnout, stress, and other negative outcomes for employees. By advocating for work-life balance and setting an example for others, Sandberg is helping to shift the culture of the tech industry and create a more sustainable, supportive work environment.

In conclusion, Sheryl Sandberg is an inspiring example of how to maintain a healthy work-life balance while pursuing a successful career. Her commitment to personal relationships, self-care, and other aspects of life beyond work has made her a role model for many people in the tech industry and beyond. Her example demonstrates that it is possible to achieve success without sacrificing other important aspects of life, and that work-life balance is crucial for personal fulfillment, productivity, and well-being.

Barack Obama is a well-known example of a successful leader who has maintained a healthy work-life balance throughout his career. Despite the demands of being President of the United States, Obama was intentional about prioritizing personal and family time, as well as pursuing his personal interests and hobbies.

Throughout his presidency, Obama was known for his love of basketball and frequently played pick-up games with staff and friends. He was also committed to staying physically fit and made time for daily workouts, often exercising in the early morning hours before starting his workday.

Obama was also intentional about spending time with his family, even during the busy and demanding schedule of the presidency. In a 2016 interview with People Magazine, he spoke about his commitment to family time, saying, "We try to make sure that when I'm in D.C., I never miss dinner with them at 6:30 PM - even if I have to go back down to the Oval Office afterward."

In addition to prioritizing personal and family time, Obama also made a point to take vacations and getaways throughout his presidency. He and his family often traveled to Hawaii for the holidays, and he was known to take short weekend trips to escape the demands of the job and recharge.

Obama's commitment to work-life balance and self-care is also evident in his post-presidency life. He has spoken publicly about the importance of taking care of oneself and pursuing personal interests, saying in a 2017 speech, "If you're not having fun, then you're not doing it right."

Obama's example shows that it is possible to achieve success in a demanding and high-pressure career while also maintaining a healthy work-life balance. By intentionally prioritizing personal and family time, pursuing personal interests and hobbies, and making time for self-care,

Obama was able to succeed in his career while also maintaining a sense of fulfillment and happiness in his personal life.

ϷϷϷ

Brian and Harvey had always dreamt of starting their own software company. When they finally took the leap, they knew that it wouldn't be easy, but they were willing to do whatever it takes to make their dream a reality. They worked hard, putting in long hours and sacrificing their personal lives for the sake of their business. But they soon realized that they needed to find a balance between their work and their personal lives.

They started by reading books on work-life balance and seeking professional help. They learned that delegation was key to reducing their workload and freeing up time for other activities. They started to delegate tasks to their team members, who were more than happy to take on additional responsibilities.

Brian and Harvey also realized the importance of taking breaks and engaging in physical activities. They started to play their favorite sports on weekends and took vacations to unwind and recharge their batteries. They found that they were more productive when they returned to work after taking some time off.

Over time, their efforts paid off, and their company began to thrive. They were able to attract new clients and secure more investments. However, their success also brought new challenges.

But they never forgot the lessons they learned along the way. They continued to prioritize work-life balance, delegating tasks to their team members, and taking time off to pursue their hobbies and interests. They found that they were able to manage their workload more efficiently and were able to make better decisions when they were well-rested and focused.

Their story became an inspiration to many others who were struggling to find the balance between work and personal life. They started receiving invitations to speak at events and conferences, and they wrote a book sharing their experiences and lessons learned.

The book became a best-seller, and people all over the world were inspired by their story. They became known as the champions of work-life balance and were recognized as leaders in their industry.

Brian and Harvey never forgot their roots, and they continued to use their success to give back to their community. They started a foundation that supports underprivileged children, providing them with education and opportunities to learn and grow.

Their story shows that with persistence, hard work, and a focus on work-life balance, anything is possible. They proved that success is not just about making money but also about creating a meaningful and fulfilling life. Their legacy lives on, inspiring others to pursue their dreams and never give up on themselves.

ᕣᕣᕣ

Achieving Work-Life Balance:

1. Set boundaries and stick to them. Decide on the hours you will work and the time you will spend on personal activities, and make sure to stick to them as much as possible.
2. Prioritize tasks and activities based on their importance and urgency. This will help you focus on what is most important and avoid getting overwhelmed.

3. Learn to say "no" when necessary. It's important to recognize your limits and not take on too much, especially if it will interfere with your personal life.
4. Make time for self-care activities such as exercise, meditation, or hobbies. These activities can help you recharge and reduce stress.
5. Seek support from family, friends, or colleagues. Building a support network can help you manage the demands of both work and personal life.

The Need to Start Now:

1. Work-life balance is essential for overall well-being and can help prevent burnout and stress-related health problems.
2. Starting early in your career can help establish healthy habits and prevent the accumulation of stress and burnout over time.
3. Achieving work-life balance can improve job satisfaction and productivity, leading to greater success and fulfillment in your career.
4. Taking care of personal needs and relationships can also lead to a happier and more fulfilling personal life.

Overall, achieving work-life balance is essential for long-term success and happiness, and it's important to start now by making intentional choices about how you spend your time and building a support network to help you manage the demands of work and personal life.

In conclusion, achieving a healthy work-life balance is essential for success and well-being. By prioritizing this habit from early career days, we can prevent burnout, increase productivity, enhance relationships, avoid regrets, and promote long-term success. It's never too early to start building habits and routines that prioritize our personal lives, and doing so can have a profound impact on our lives and careers.

ppp

Chapter Summary:

In this chapter, we explored the importance of achieving a healthy work-life balance and its impact on career success and overall well-being. We learned that before the Industrial Revolution, work was more closely tied to the community and family life, with flexible schedules and integrated work and leisure activities. However, with the rise of industrialization, work-life balance was disrupted, leading to long working hours and a separation between work and personal life.

We discussed the negative effects of the Industrial Revolution on work-life balance, including the focus on profits over employee well-being and the prevalence of long work hours and irregular schedules. We explored how this imbalance has persisted in modern times, with companies still prioritizing productivity over personal well-being.

Furthermore, we examined the importance of aligning work with natural rhythms and the negative consequences of working outside of these cycles. The disruption of the circadian rhythm can lead to a variety of health problems, both physical and mental, and chronic overwork and stress can have severe consequences for our well-being.

The chapter emphasized the benefits of a healthy work-life balance, including the prevention of burnout, increased productivity, improved relationships, and the avoidance of regrets later in life. We learned that prioritizing personal lives and engaging in non-work activities can enhance overall productivity and job satisfaction.

Activity:

1. *Reflect on your current work-life balance: Take a moment to assess how you currently balance your work and personal life. Identify areas where adjustments may be needed to create a healthier balance.*
2. *Set clear boundaries: Establish specific hours for work and personal activities to avoid blending them together. Avoid checking work-related emails or engaging in work tasks during designated personal time.*
3. *Prioritize self-care: Make time for activities that help you relax and rejuvenate, such as exercise, meditation, hobbies, or spending time in nature. Schedule regular self-care practices to ensure your physical and mental well-being.*
4. *Delegate and ask for support: Identify tasks that can be delegated at work or home to lighten your workload. Seek support from colleagues, friends, or family members to share responsibilities and create more time for yourself.*
5. *Establish a technology routine: Limit the use of technology outside of work hours to prevent constant connectivity. Designate specific times or zones for disconnecting from devices and focus on personal activities.*
6. *Plan and prioritize: Utilize effective time management techniques, such as creating to-do lists or using productivity tools, to stay organized and ensure that you allocate time for both work and personal commitments.*

By implementing these strategies, you can take important steps toward achieving a healthier work-life balance, leading to increased well-being, reduced stress, and a more fulfilling life.

ϼϼϼ

TWELVE

Awakening the True Self: The Journey of Self-Realization

———❦———

"The state we call realization is simply being oneself, not knowing anything or becoming anything." - Sri Ramana Maharshi

❦❦❦

Self-realization is the process of understanding and accepting oneself, including one's strengths, weaknesses, values, and beliefs. It is a crucial aspect of personal growth and development, and can have a profound impact on one's ability to achieve success.

To begin with, self-realization enables individuals to identify their unique talents and strengths, and to pursue careers and goals that align with their skills and interests. When individuals have a clear understanding of their abilities and passions, they are better able to set goals and make decisions that are in line with their personal values and aspirations. This, in turn, can lead to greater job satisfaction, fulfillment, and success.

Moreover, self-realization allows individuals to identify their weaknesses and limitations, and to work towards overcoming them. By acknowledging their areas for improvement, individuals can take steps to develop new skills, seek out learning opportunities, and take on new challenges. This can help them to become more well-rounded and adaptable, and can enhance their ability to succeed in a variety of situations.

Self-realization also enables individuals to develop a greater sense of self-awareness and emotional intelligence. By understanding their own thoughts, feelings, and motivations, individuals can better manage their own emotions and reactions, and can also develop more empathy and understanding towards others. This can be particularly important in leadership roles, where emotional intelligence is often seen as a key attribute of success.

In addition, self-realization can help individuals to develop more effective communication skills. By understanding their own communication style and preferences, individuals can learn to adapt their approach to better connect with others and convey their ideas and messages. This can be particularly important in the workplace, where effective communication is often crucial to success.

Finally, self-realization can lead to greater self-confidence and resilience. When individuals have a clear sense of their own identity and purpose, they are less likely to be swayed by external pressures or criticism, and are better able to bounce back from setbacks and failures. This can help them to maintain their motivation and focus, and to persevere in the face of challenges and obstacles.

Self-realization is a critical component of personal and professional success. By understanding and accepting oneself, individuals can identify their unique talents and passions, overcome their weaknesses, develop emotional intelligence and effective communication skills, and build confidence and resilience. These qualities can help individuals to achieve their goals and make a positive impact in their personal and professional lives.

Self-Realization Spiritually

Self-realization spiritually refers to the process of discovering and understanding your true nature and connection to a higher power or consciousness. It involves a deep exploration of your beliefs, values, and purpose in life, and can be achieved through practices such as meditation, mindfulness, and self-reflection. This type of self-realization is often associated with spiritual growth and enlightenment, and is focused on achieving inner peace, harmony, and a sense of oneness with the universe.

Swami Vivekananda was a spiritual leader and philosopher from India who played a key role in the introduction of Vedanta and Yoga in the western world. His teachings continue to inspire millions of people around the world, and his emphasis on self-realization, the pursuit of knowledge and truth, and the importance of service to others remain relevant even today.

One of the key teachings of Swami Vivekananda was the idea of self-realization. He believed that the ultimate goal of human life was to realize our true nature, which is divine. He taught that this realization can be achieved through the practice of meditation, self-discipline, and devotion to a higher power. Swami Vivekananda believed that once we achieve self-realization, we will be free from all limitations and attain ultimate peace and happiness.

Another important teaching of Swami Vivekananda was the pursuit of knowledge and truth. He believed that the pursuit of knowledge was essential for the development of a person's character and the advancement of society. He encouraged people to be curious, to question everything, and to seek knowledge from all sources. He believed that the pursuit of truth was essential for spiritual growth and for the betterment of society.

Swami Vivekananda also emphasized the importance of service to others. He believed that serving others was the highest form of worship and that it was the duty of every person to help those in need. He believed that service to others was not just a moral obligation but also a means of self-purification and spiritual growth.

In addition to these teachings, Swami Vivekananda also emphasized the importance of living a simple and humble life. He believed that material possessions and worldly pleasures were temporary and that true happiness could only be achieved through spiritual growth and the realization of the divine within oneself.

Swami Vivekananda's teachings continue to inspire people around the world, and his message of self-realization, the pursuit of knowledge and truth, and service to others remains relevant even today. His teachings are a reminder of the importance of living a life of purpose and meaning and of the power of spiritual growth and self-realization.

To summarize, Swami Vivekananda's teachings can be distilled into the following key points:

1. The ultimate goal of human life is self-realization, which can be achieved through the practice of meditation, self-discipline, and devotion to a higher power.
2. The pursuit of knowledge and truth is essential for spiritual growth and for the betterment of society.
3. Service to others is the highest form of worship and is essential for self-purification and spiritual growth.
4. Living a simple and humble life is important for spiritual growth and the realization of true happiness.

Bob Marley, the legendary reggae musician, experienced a significant transformation in his music after a powerful self-realization experience. In the late 1970s, Marley was at the height of his career, with millions of fans around the world and a reputation as a powerful and passionate performer. But despite his success, Marley was struggling with personal issues and searching for deeper meaning in his life.

In 1978, Marley was diagnosed with melanoma, a serious form of skin cancer. This diagnosis forced him to confront his own mortality and sparked a period of intense self-reflection. During this time, Marley began to explore his spiritual beliefs and to seek out a deeper connection with his African roots.

Marley's newfound self-awareness had a profound impact on his music. He began to infuse his lyrics with themes of social justice, political activism, and spiritual awakening. Songs like "War" and "Redemption Song" reflected his deep commitment to the struggle for human rights and his belief in the power of unity and love to overcome oppression.

Marley's music became a platform for spreading his message of peace, love, and social justice to the world. He used his celebrity status to promote causes he believed in, including the fight against apartheid in South Africa and the struggle for independence in Zimbabwe. Through his music and activism, Marley became a symbol of hope and inspiration for millions of people around the world.

Marley's self-realization experience transformed not only his music but also his personal life. He became a more compassionate and empathetic person, and his commitment to social justice and equality continued to shape his life and work until his untimely death in 1981.

Marley's journey serves as a powerful example of the transformative power of self-realization. By confronting his own mortality and seeking out a deeper connection with his spirituality, Marley was able to tap into his truest self and to use his music as a vehicle for positive change in the world.

Alexander the Great was a famous ancient Greek king and military leader who is known for his conquests and his empire that spanned from Greece to India. During his last days, Alexander experienced a profound self-realization that changed his perspective on life and his legacy. He realized that his material wealth and power were not enough to bring him true happiness or satisfaction, and that his actions had caused immense suffering and loss of life for many people. Alexander became deeply introspective and began to reflect on his life and his purpose. He realized that his legacy should be one of peace and understanding, rather than conquest and war.

Alexander's self-realization led him to make some important decisions, including the abandonment of his plans to conquer more territories and the adoption of a more conciliatory approach towards his enemies. He also began to focus more on spreading Greek culture and philosophy, rather than simply expanding his empire. Unfortunately, Alexander's self-realization came too late, as he died shortly thereafter, leaving behind a legacy that was both controversial and complex. Nevertheless, his realization serves as an important reminder of the power of self-reflection and the need to prioritize our inner growth and personal development over external achievements and material possessions.

Ashoka was a powerful ruler of the Mauryan Empire in India, who after the devastating Kalinga War in 261 BCE, underwent a transformation that led to his self-realization. Before the war, Ashoka was known for his violent and ruthless methods of expansion and conquest, but the horrific casualties of the Kalinga War, including thousands of dead and injured soldiers and civilians, left a deep impact on him.

After the war, Ashoka realized the futility of war and conquest and became a proponent of nonviolence, compassion, and moral righteousness. He converted to Buddhism, which he felt embodied these values, and started promoting it throughout his empire. He became known as "Dhammashoka" or Ashoka the Righteous, and his reign became an era of peace, prosperity, and social welfare.

Ashoka's self-realization and transformation are evident in his famous edicts, inscribed on pillars and rocks throughout the empire. These edicts encourage the principles of nonviolence, tolerance, and respect for all living beings. He also ordered the construction of hospitals, rest houses, and other public amenities, and encouraged the spread of education, art, and culture.

Ashoka's self-realization journey is a prime example of how an individual's perspective and actions can transform after experiencing a life-altering event. His realization that violence and war only lead to suffering and destruction, and that peace, compassion, and morality are essential for a happy and prosperous society, left a lasting impact on India and the world.

On the other hand, self-realization of potential to succeed refers to the process of identifying and maximizing your personal abilities and talents to achieve your goals and aspirations. It involves a deep understanding of your strengths and weaknesses, and the development of the skills and knowledge needed to succeed in your chosen field or career. This type of self-realization is often associated with personal growth and career advancement, and is focused on achieving external success, recognition, and accomplishment.

Self-realization is a fascinating and complex topic that can take us on a journey of self-discovery and understanding. It involves delving deep into our inner selves and exploring our beliefs, values, and purpose in life. However, in this book, we will be focusing on self-realization in the context of personal growth and career advancement.

It's important to note that self-realization can take many forms, including spiritual, emotional, and intellectual. However, for the purpose of this book, we will be discussing the aspect of self-realization that pertains to achieving our full potential in our chosen career or field.

When we talk about self-realization in terms of career or personal growth, we are referring to the process of identifying and maximizing our personal abilities and talents to achieve our goals and aspirations. This process involves a deep understanding of our strengths and weaknesses, as well as the development of the skills and knowledge needed to succeed in our chosen field.

Self-Realization of Potential

Self-realization of potential to succeed is focused on achieving external success, recognition, and accomplishment. It involves setting and achieving goals, overcoming challenges, and continually striving to be the best version of ourselves.

While this type of self-realization may not seem as profound or spiritual as the concept of achieving inner peace and oneness with the universe, it can still be a deeply fulfilling and rewarding experience. By unlocking our full potential and achieving success in our chosen field, we can create a sense of purpose and meaning in our lives, and contribute to the betterment of the world around us.

Andrew Carnegie, one of the most successful entrepreneurs of the 19th century, is a prime example of the power of self-realization. He was a self-made man who began his career as a telegraph operator and worked his way up to become a successful industrialist, philanthropist, and one of the wealthiest men in American history.

One of the key aspects of Carnegie's success was his ability to recognize his own strengths and weaknesses. He realized early on that he was not a skilled engineer or mechanic, and that he needed to surround himself with people who possessed those skills if he wanted to succeed in the steel industry.

Instead of trying to learn all the necessary skills himself, Carnegie made it his mission to hire the best engineers, mechanics, and other skilled workers he could find. By doing so, he was able to create a team of experts who were able to design and build some of the most advanced and efficient steel mills in the world.

Carnegie's focus on hiring the best talent was a key factor in his success. He understood that he didn't need to be an expert in everything, but that he could leverage the skills of others to achieve his goals. By doing so, he was able to build a highly successful business that revolutionized the steel industry and made him one of the wealthiest men in history.

Carnegie's approach to self-realization is a valuable lesson for anyone looking to achieve success in their chosen field. By recognizing our own strengths and weaknesses, and surrounding ourselves with people who possess the skills and expertise we lack, we can create a team of experts that can achieve great things. This approach not only maximizes our chances of success, but it also allows us to focus on the areas where we excel and make the greatest impact.

ppp

Brian and Harvey had poured in all their energy into building the business, working long hours and taking on new projects. Their hard work had paid off and they were successful with initial fundings and were enjoying a decent success of their company.

However, despite their early success, Brian and Harvey soon realized that they were not growing at the intended rate. They knew they needed to do something different to take the company to the next level.

It was then that they had a moment of self-realization. They both knew they were technical coders at heart, but they didn't have the business acumen or leadership skills to take the company to the next level. They needed a CEO who could run the business and help them achieve their goals.

So, they set out to find the right person for the job. After a long search, they finally found a famous name in the industry, someone who had a track record of turning companies around and growing them into market leaders.

The new CEO brought a wealth of experience and expertise to the table, and he immediately set to work transforming the company. He implemented new processes, streamlined operations, and focused on building a strong sales and marketing team.

Within just five years, the company had grown exponentially. They had expanded into new markets, launched new products, and had become one of the most successful software companies in the industry.

Brian and Harvey were overjoyed at the success of their company, and they knew that it wouldn't have been possible without their self-realization that they needed a CEO to help them grow. They were proud of the company they had built and the team they had assembled, and they knew that their future was bright.

ᗡᗡᗡ

Self-realization is the key to success in both personal and professional life. Andrew Carnegie and Brian and Harvey are great examples of how self-realization helped them in achieving their goals. Carnegie was able to identify his strengths and weaknesses, which allowed him to surround himself with the right people to help him achieve his goals. Similarly, Brian and Harvey realized that their strength was coding and not business, which helped them to address the arising issue and move towards the path of growth.

However, sometimes our ego comes in between, preventing us from accepting our weaknesses. It is important to overcome this and move forward, identifying our shortcomings and working on them. Today, collaboration is the game-changer in the business world, and there are numerous examples of successful collaborations that have helped companies grow.

One such example is the Nike and Apple partnership. In 2006, these two major brands came together to combine Nike's sports expertise with Apple's technology to create a seamless experience for fitness enthusiasts. The partnership resulted in the creation of the Nike+ platform, which allowed users to track their workouts using Apple devices and Nike accessories.

Collaboration is the key to success in today's world, and partnerships like these are vital for growth and success. By dropping our ego and accepting our strengths and weaknesses, we can work towards achieving our goals and collaborating with others to achieve even greater success. So take the first step towards self-realization today, identify your strengths and weaknesses, and start working towards achieving your full potential.

Albert Einstein was born on March 14, 1879, in Ulm, a small town in Germany. As a child, Einstein was curious and had an early interest in science. He was an average student in his early years and had difficulty in following the traditional educational system. At the age of 16, Einstein left high school without a diploma and applied to the Swiss Federal Institute of Technology (ETH) in Zurich, but he failed the entrance examination. He then enrolled in a school in Aarau, Switzerland, where he was able to complete his secondary education. After graduation, he applied to the ETH again and was admitted to the

Mathematics and Physics program in 1896.

At ETH, Einstein had a difficult time adjusting to the traditional teaching methods, and he often skipped classes to study physics and mathematics on his own. Despite this, he excelled in his studies and graduated in 1900 with a degree in mathematics and physics. However, he was unable to secure a teaching position and instead took a job as a technical assistant in the Swiss Patent Office in Bern in 1902. It was during his time at the Patent Office that he was able to pursue his scientific interests, and he began publishing papers on his groundbreaking theories of relativity.

Albert Einstein's journey is a testament to the power of self-realization.

Einstein's story reminds us that even the most profound discoveries can begin with humble beginnings. Einstein's journey started when he became a patent clerk in Bern, Switzerland. It was here that he began to question the fundamental assumptions of classical physics and started to explore the concept of time and space. He worked tirelessly on his research, never giving up on his quest for knowledge.

Einstein's "miracle year" papers in 1905 introduced the theory of special relativity, which changed our understanding of time and space forever. He continued to work on his theories, and in 1915, he published his groundbreaking theory of general relativity, which expanded on the principles of special relativity to include gravity.

Einstein's self-realization journey allowed him to make groundbreaking discoveries that transformed our understanding of the universe. He never stopped questioning the world around him, and he remained humble despite his significant achievements. Einstein's story reminds us that self-realization is a lifelong journey, and we should never stop questioning and seeking knowledge.

Through self-realization, we can overcome limiting beliefs, embrace our unique talents and abilities, and make meaningful contributions to the world. It requires courage, persistence, and a willingness to embrace change and uncertainty. But the rewards of self-realization are immense, leading to personal growth, fulfillment, and the ability to create positive change in the world around us.

The journey of self-realization is not easy, but it is necessary for anyone seeking to live a fulfilling and purposeful life. We must take the time to question our assumptions and beliefs, confront our fears, and embrace our true selves. As Einstein once said, "The important thing is not to stop questioning. Curiosity has its own reason for existing."

ÞÞÞ

Chapter Summary:

In this chapter, we explored the concept of self-realization and its impact on personal growth and success. We delved into the journey of self-discovery and understanding, as individuals sought to identify and accept their true selves. We discussed how self-realization enables individuals to align their careers and goals with their passions and values, leading to greater satisfaction and fulfillment. Additionally, we explored how self-realization helps individuals recognize their weaknesses and work towards overcoming them, fostering adaptability and success in various situations. We also highlighted the importance of self-awareness, emotional intelligence, and effective communication skills in building a strong personal brand. Furthermore, we emphasized the significance of seeking feedback, evolving and adapting, and consistently delivering value to establish and maintain a successful personal brand. By following these principles, individuals can systematically build their personal brand, positioning themselves for success and opening doors to new opportunities.

Activity:

After reading the chapter on self-realization, here is an activity that readers can engage in to further their journey of self-discovery and personal growth:

1. Set aside dedicated time in your schedule for self-reflection. Find a quiet and comfortable space where you can focus and reflect without distractions.
2. Take out a journal or notebook and divide it into four sections: Strengths, Weaknesses, Values and Beliefs, and Goals.
3. Begin with the Strengths section. Reflect on your unique talents, skills, and abilities. Write down at least five strengths that you possess and think about how you can leverage them to pursue your passions and achieve your goals.
4. Move on to the Weaknesses section. Be honest with yourself and identify areas where you can improve or develop new skills. Write down at least five weaknesses

or limitations that you recognize in yourself. Consider how you can address these weaknesses and what steps you can take to overcome them.

5. In the Values and Beliefs section, reflect on your core values and beliefs. Think about what truly matters to you and what principles guide your decisions and actions. Write down your values and beliefs, and consider how they align with your goals and aspirations.

6. Finally, in the Goals section, identify both short-term and long-term goals that are meaningful to you. Consider how your strengths, weaknesses, values, and beliefs can inform and shape your goals. Write down specific, achievable goals that resonate with your authentic self.

7. After completing the journaling activity, take a moment to review what you have written. Reflect on the insights gained and consider how they can influence your personal and professional life moving forward.

Remember, self-reflection is an ongoing process. You can revisit your journal periodically to track your progress, reassess your goals, and make adjustments as needed. This activity will help you deepen your understanding of yourself, clarify your aspirations, and set a clear path towards personal and professional success based on your unique strengths and values.

ﬤﬤﬤ

THIRTEEN

PERSONAL BRANDING: CREATING YOUR OWN IDENTITY

"Your brand is what people say about you when you're not in the room." - Jeff Bezos.

Picture yourself walking through a crowded market in a foreign city, searching for that perfect souvenir to take home with you. You come across two vendors selling the same item, but you can't help but feel a sense of uncertainty. How do you know which vendor to trust? This is where personal branding becomes essential.

On one side of the market, there's a vendor selling their product with no visible branding or personal touch. On the other side, a vendor has built his personal brand with a business card, a buy-back offer, and a challenge to prove the authenticity of his product. You can't help but be intrigued by the second vendor's personal branding.

As you approach the second vendor, he confidently hands you his business card, introducing himself and his product with a warm smile. You can't help but feel more at ease knowing that you can contact him directly if any issues arise. Then, he offers you a buy-back option within 24 hours, which immediately shows his confidence in the authenticity of his product.

But the most exciting part is when he challenges you to prove the authenticity of his product. Your curiosity piqued, you decide to take him up on his offer. He expertly demonstrates the unique features of his product, and you can't help but feel impressed by his knowledge and confidence.

By the end of the interaction, you've not only purchased a high-quality product but also developed a sense of trust in the vendor's personal brand. The experience has left you feeling satisfied, excited, and intrigued by the power of personal branding.

This is the power of personal branding in sales. It not only sets you apart from others but also establishes you as a trusted authority in your industry. It's about showcasing your skills, strengths, and values in a way that positions you as an expert in your field.

Personal branding is critical in today's competitive world, where thousands of candidates are vying for the same opportunities. Whether you're applying for a job, trying to secure admission to a university, or preparing for an interview, it's crucial to differentiate yourself from the competition. Building a personal brand allows you to showcase your unique strengths, skills, and values in a way that resonates with potential employers or institutions.

By developing a strong personal brand, you can differentiate yourself from others and build lasting relationships with those around you. It allows you to connect with people on a deeper level, and showcase your expertise and value in a way that inspires trust and respect.

Personal branding is not just for entrepreneurs or sales representatives, it is applicable to anyone looking to elevate their professional and personal life. By focusing on building your personal brand, you can position yourself for success and open doors to new opportunities.

In today's competitive world, standing out from the crowd has become more important than ever. Whether you're a business owner, a freelancer, or a job seeker, creating a unique personal brand can help you to differentiate yourself and elevate your career. Personal branding is the practice of intentionally crafting an identity, image, and reputation for yourself that showcases your skills, strengths, and values in a way that sets you apart from others in your field.

To create a personal brand that truly reflects who you are and what you have to offer, you need to start with self-reflection. Take the time to identify your core values, passions, and unique strengths. What do you love to do? What are you really good at? What sets you apart from others in your field? Answering these questions will help you to develop a clear understanding of your personal brand and what you want to communicate to your target audience.

Why is Personal Branding Important?

Personal branding is important for a number of reasons. First, it allows you to differentiate yourself from others in your industry. With so many people vying for the same jobs and opportunities, it's important to establish a unique and compelling brand that sets you apart from the crowd.

Second, a strong personal brand helps to establish your credibility and expertise in your field. By sharing your knowledge and insights through thought leadership, speaking engagements, or other means, you can demonstrate to others that you are an authority in your industry.

Finally, a personal brand can help you to create new opportunities for career advancement. By establishing yourself as a thought leader or expert in your field, you may be approached with new job offers, speaking engagements, or other opportunities that can help you to grow your career.

Key Components of a Strong Personal Brand

To establish a strong personal brand, there are a number of key components to consider. These include:

A clear value proposition: Your personal brand should be built around a clear and compelling value proposition that sets you apart from your peers. This may include your unique skills, strengths, and areas of expertise.

A strong online presence: In today's digital age, having a strong online presence is essential for building a personal brand. This can include creating a professional website or blog, actively participating in social media, and developing a strong LinkedIn profile.

Effective networking: Building strong relationships with colleagues, mentors, and other professionals is critical for establishing oneself as a brand. Attend industry events, join professional organizations, and seek out opportunities to connect with others in your field.

Thought leadership: To establish oneself as a brand, it's important to become a thought leader in your industry. This can be achieved by regularly publishing articles or blog posts on relevant topics, speaking at industry conferences, or participating in panel discussions.

Consistency: To build a strong personal brand, it's important to maintain consistency across all aspects of your professional life. This includes maintaining a consistent message, tone, and image in all communications and interactions.

Personal branding is an essential aspect of modern life, but it can be tricky to get right. Many people feel the pressure to present themselves in a certain way, whether to impress others or to fit in with a particular group. However, it is important to remember that personal branding should be an authentic representation of who you are, and not an embellished or fabricated version of yourself. When you build a personal brand on false claims or exaggerations, it may help you in the short term, but it is likely to come back and bite you in the long run.

An exaggerated personal branding example could be something like claiming to have climbed Mount Everest without any prior mountaineering experience or training. While it may seem impressive to others, it's not only false but also dangerous to claim such feats without any basis. These are exaggerated claims that may impress others initially, but they are unlikely to be sustainable in the long run. Similarly, falsely claiming to have a higher education degree or to have achieved a certain level of financial success may impress people at first, but the truth will eventually come out.

In fact, building a personal brand on lies and false stories can actually be detrimental to your success. It can erode trust and credibility, making it difficult to build lasting relationships or gain the respect of others. Worse yet, it can damage your reputation and harm your chances of future success.

So, when building your personal brand, stay true to your values and only present yourself in ways that you can live up to. Be honest about your accomplishments, your strengths, and your weaknesses. Remember, your personal brand is a reflection of who you are, and it should be a genuine and authentic representation of your true self.

The Mahabharata is a Hindu epic that tells the story of the Kuru dynasty and the great war between the Kauravas and the Pandavas. During the course of the story, the kingdom of Matsya, ruled by King Virat, was attacked by the Kuru army.

In the kingdom of Matsya, Prince Uttar was known for boasting about his bravery, even though he had never actually faced any real danger. He would often tell tales of his heroic exploits, exaggerating his achievements and creating a false image of himself as a courageous warrior.

When the Kuru army attacked Matsya, Uttar was suddenly called upon to defend his kingdom. He found himself facing real danger for the first time, and his false reputation was quickly exposed. Despite being accompanied by the Pandava prince Arjuna, who was in disguise as a eunuch dancer named Brihannala, Uttar was unable to live up to the expectations that he had created for himself. In the face of real danger, Uttar's bravado and false confidence crumbled, and he fled from the battle in fear, abandoning his people and his kingdom.

The attack on Matsya by the Kuru army was a significant event in the Mahabharata, as it set the stage for the eventual war between the Kauravas and the Pandavas.

Uttar's story serves as a cautionary tale about the dangers of creating a false image of ourselves, and the importance of being honest with ourselves and others about our strengths and weaknesses.

In the world of business, there are always stories of both success and failure. One such story serves as a cautionary tale for those looking to build their own brand. A once-promising company, valued at a staggering $9 billion, had claimed to have revolutionized blood testing. The company's founder, a highly regarded entrepreneur, was hailed as the youngest and wealthiest self-made female billionaire in the country. However, doubts soon emerged about the accuracy of the technology and the claims made by the company.

As investigations began to uncover the truth, it became clear that the company had built its brand on false and fabricated stories and claims. The founder was accused of misleading investors and the government, and was charged with raising $700 million through false and exaggerated claims. In the end, the truth about the company was revealed, and the founder was convicted of fraud.

This story underscores the importance of building brands with truth, integrity, and honesty. While it may be tempting to exaggerate the capabilities and accomplishments of a business, doing so can ultimately lead to failure and disappointment. Instead, businesses should focus on delivering real value to their customers and stakeholders, building their brand on a foundation of trust and authenticity. By doing so, they can earn the respect and loyalty of their customers, and achieve lasting success.

There are many individuals who have successfully established themselves as a brand in their industry. Here are a few examples:

Seth Godin is a renowned marketing expert, author, and entrepreneur who is widely regarded as a pioneer in the field of personal branding. His career is a testament to the power of personal branding and how it can be used to build a successful career.

Seth Godin started his career in traditional marketing, working for companies such as Spinnaker Software and Yoyodyne. However, he soon realized that he wanted to do something different and decided to start his own company. He founded Seth Godin Productions in 1986, a book packaging company that created books and multimedia products for publishers. The company became a success, and Seth Godin gained recognition as a talented marketer and entrepreneur.

However, Seth Godin's real breakthrough came in the early 2000s, when he started blogging. He used his blog as a platform to share his thoughts and ideas on marketing, leadership, and entrepreneurship. His blog, called Seth's Blog, became one of the most popular and influential blogs in the world, with millions of readers.

Through his blog, Seth Godin established himself as a thought leader in the marketing industry. He shared his unique insights and ideas on marketing and branding, and his readers looked up to him for guidance and inspiration. He used his blog to build his personal brand and establish himself as an authority in his field.

Seth Godin's personal branding efforts didn't stop there. He has written over 20 books, many of which have become bestsellers. His books are known for their unique insights and practical advice on marketing, leadership, and entrepreneurship. His books have helped him establish himself as a leading authority in the marketing industry, and they have helped him build a loyal following of readers who look up to him for guidance and inspiration.

Seth Godin's personal branding efforts have also extended to public speaking. He is a sought-after speaker and has spoken at conferences and events around the world. His speeches are known for their unique insights and practical advice on marketing and leadership. He uses his public speaking engagements to further establish his personal brand and share his ideas with a wider audience.

Through his personal branding efforts, Seth Godin has built a successful career as a marketing expert, author, and entrepreneur. He has established himself as a thought leader in the marketing industry, and his insights and ideas are widely respected and sought-after. His personal brand has helped him build a loyal following of readers and customers who trust and respect him.

Seth Godin's case study demonstrates the power of personal branding and how it can be used to build a successful career. By developing a clear value proposition, building a strong online presence, establishing thought leadership, and maintaining consistency, individuals can establish themselves as a brand in their industry and create new opportunities for career success

Tim Ferriss is a well-known personal brand in the business and self-help industry. He is an entrepreneur, investor, and author who rose to fame after publishing his bestselling book, "The 4-Hour Workweek."

Ferriss' personal branding journey started with the publication of his book. He had a clear value proposition: to help people improve their work-life balance and achieve more in less time. He built a strong online presence by creating a blog and podcast, where he shared his ideas and thoughts on entrepreneurship, productivity, and lifestyle design.

Ferriss used his online platforms to establish thought leadership in his industry. He interviewed successful entrepreneurs, authors, and business leaders and shared their insights with his followers. By doing so, he became a trusted authority in his field and gained a massive following of people who looked up to him for guidance and advice.

Ferriss also maintained consistency in his personal branding efforts. He continued to publish books, create podcasts, and speak at events, consistently delivering valuable content to his audience. He also leveraged his personal brand to create new opportunities for career success, such as investing in startups and launching his own products.

One of the keys to Ferriss' personal branding success was his ability to connect with his audience on a personal level. He shared his personal struggles and failures, making him relatable to his followers. He also encouraged two-way communication by responding to comments and engaging with his audience on social media.

Ferriss' personal branding efforts have paid off immensely. He has become a New York Times bestselling author, a popular podcaster, and a sought-after speaker. He has also invested in companies such as Uber, Twitter, and Alibaba, and launched his own products such as the "4-Hour Body" and "4-Hour Chef" books.

Overall, Tim Ferriss is an excellent example of the power of personal branding. By developing a clear value proposition, building a strong online presence, establishing thought leadership, maintaining consistency, and connecting with his audience on a personal level, Ferriss has become a trusted authority in his industry and created new opportunities for career success.

Let's summarize the key points that can help you establish a strong personal brand based on your work:

1. Identify your unique value proposition: What sets you apart from others in your industry or field? Identify your strengths, skills, and expertise, and develop a clear value proposition that communicates what you can offer.

2. Build a strong online presence: In today's digital age, having a strong online presence is crucial to establishing your personal brand. Create a website or blog that showcases your work and expertise, and use social media platforms to connect with others in your industry and share your insights.

3. Network effectively: Building relationships with others in your industry is important for establishing your personal brand. Attend conferences and industry events, join professional organizations, and engage with others on social media to expand your network.

4. Establish thought leadership: Establish yourself as a thought leader in your industry by sharing your knowledge and insights through speaking engagements, writing articles or blog posts, and creating educational content.

5. Maintain consistency: Consistency is key when it comes to personal branding. Ensure that your message, image, and overall brand remain consistent across all of your online and offline platforms.

By following these key steps, you can establish a strong personal brand that sets you apart from others in your industry and helps you achieve success in life.

ϷϷϷ

Brian and Harvey had been seasoned professionals in the software industry, having worked on various projects after graduating from college. They had gained extensive knowledge and experience, and their passion for technology had led them to start their own software company. Despite their expertise, they faced challenges in building their personal branding and establishing their company as a trusted brand in the industry.

At the start, they struggled to convince potential customers to trust them and their new company. Their lack of personal branding made it challenging to attract new clients, and they found themselves competing with established companies in the industry. They realized that they needed to build their personal brand to establish trust and credibility with their customers.

Brian and Harvey started by being honest and transparent about their work and values. They shared their knowledge and expertise on social media platforms and attended industry events to connect with other professionals. They also focused on delivering quality work and providing excellent customer service, which helped them build a positive reputation in the industry.

As they continued to build their personal brand, they also worked on establishing their company as a trusted brand. They focused on creating products that were innovative and met the needs of their customers. They also built a team of professionals who shared their values and commitment to excellence.

Their efforts paid off when they landed a major contract with a large tech company. Their reputation for quality work and integrity had preceded them, and they were able to secure the contract over more established competitors.

From there, their company continued to grow, and they became known as a reliable and innovative software company.

Brian and Harvey's story demonstrates the importance of building a personal brand and establishing a company brand based on truth, integrity, and morals. By being honest, transparent, and committed to excellence, they were able to overcome initial challenges and build a successful software company. In today's competitive world, personal branding and establishing a trusted company brand are essential for success in any industry.

ppp

Chapter Summary:

In this chapter, we explored the importance of personal branding in today's competitive world and how it can help you stand out from the crowd. We discussed the key components of a strong personal brand, including a clear value proposition, a strong online presence, effective networking, thought leadership, and consistency. We emphasized the need for authenticity and honesty in building a personal brand, cautioning against the dangers of exaggerating or fabricating claims. We shared cautionary tales from both ancient epics and real-life business scenarios, highlighting the consequences of building a brand on false stories or misleading information. We also examined the success stories of renowned individuals like Seth Godin and Tim Ferriss, who effectively utilized personal branding to establish themselves as thought leaders in their industries. Finally, we provided practical steps for building a strong personal brand, such as identifying your unique value proposition, building an online presence, networking effectively, establishing thought leadership, and maintaining consistency. By following these steps, you can create a personal brand that differentiates you from others, builds credibility and trust, and opens doors to new opportunities.

Activity Plan:

1. *Self-Reflection: Identify your core values, passions, and unique strengths.*
2. *Define Your Value Proposition: Clearly articulate your unique skills, strengths, and areas of expertise.*
3. *Create an Online Presence: Develop a professional website or blog and engage on relevant social media platforms.*
4. *Network Effectively: Attend industry events, join professional organizations, and seek mentorship.*
5. *Establish Thought Leadership: Publish articles, seek speaking engagements, and contribute to relevant publications.*
6. *Maintain Consistency: Ensure a consistent message, tone, and image across all communications.*
7. *Seek Feedback and Iterate: Request feedback and use it to refine and improve your personal brand.*
8. *Evolve and Adapt: Stay informed about industry trends and continuously enhance your expertise.*
9. *Monitor and Manage Your Online Presence: Regularly review and update your online profiles and address any negative feedback.*
10. *Consistently Deliver Value: Focus on providing exceptional service and valuable insights to your target audience.*

By following these points, you can systematically build and strengthen your personal brand, positioning yourself for success and opening doors to new opportunities in your professional life.

• 241 •

ᗡᗡᗡ

FOURTEEN

GIVING CREDITS: THE ART OF ACKNOWLEDGING

"I've learned that people will forget what you said, people will forget what you did, but people will never forget how you made them feel." - Maya Angelou.

Have you ever wondered why, when famous personalities, achievers, celebrities or sports personnel win an award or are honored, they tend to thank a multitude of people in their lives for their success? Why is it so important for them to acknowledge the efforts of others? Well, let's delve into this together and explore the reasons why we should acknowledge and give due credit to the people around us in order to succeed.

Have you ever achieved something significant in your life? Take a moment to reflect on that accomplishment. Now, think about the people who supported you along the way. Did you have mentors or role models who provided guidance and wisdom? Did you receive assistance from friends, family, or colleagues? Chances are, your success wasn't solely due to your individual efforts. It involved a network of people who played a part in your journey. When we acknowledge and give credit to these individuals, we not only express gratitude but also recognize the collaborative nature of success.

Have you ever considered the power of interconnectedness? Our lives are not solitary endeavors. We are all part of a vast web of relationships and connections. Think about the opportunities that have come your way. How many of them were a result of someone else's influence or assistance? By acknowledging and giving credit to the people who have supported us, we honor the interconnectedness of our lives. We acknowledge that our achievements are not isolated events but rather a culmination of collective efforts.

Have you ever thought about the impact of acknowledging others on your relationships? When we express gratitude and give credit where it is due, we strengthen the bonds we share with those who have helped us along the way. Think about the joy and satisfaction you feel when someone acknowledges your contribution. Now imagine how that acknowledgment can deepen the connection between you and the people who have supported your success. By acknowledging others, we create a positive cycle of support and encouragement.

Have you ever recognized your own limitations and the fallacy of self-sufficiency? As much as we would like to believe that we can achieve success on our own, the truth is that we all have our areas of expertise and our limitations. Acknowledging the contributions of others reminds us that we are not alone. It encourages us to seek assistance and guidance when needed, leveraging the collective wisdom and experience of those around us. By acknowledging and giving credit to others, we create a support system that strengthens our strengths and compensates for our weaknesses.

Have you ever considered the impact of acknowledging others on creating a positive and inclusive culture? Success is not limited to a single person or a select few. It is the result of diverse contributions from individuals with different backgrounds and perspectives. When we acknowledge and give credit to this diverse group, we foster an environment where everyone feels valued and appreciated. In turn, this encourages collaboration and innovation, as people are more likely to freely share their ideas and work together towards common goals.

Have you ever contemplated the power of abundance over scarcity? Acknowledging others' contributions dispels the notion that someone else's success diminishes our own. It promotes the belief that there is enough success to go around. By celebrating the achievements of others and recognizing their contributions, we create an atmosphere of support and encouragement. This mindset of abundance not only fuels our motivation but also opens doors to new opportunities and collaborations that may have otherwise remained closed.

In the grand tapestry of success, every thread counts. Each person who has played a role in our journey deserves to be acknowledged and credited. From mentors and teachers who have imparted their knowledge to colleagues and friends who have offered their support, these individuals have made an indelible impact on our path to success. So, as you strive for your own goals and accomplishments, remember the power of acknowledging and giving credit to the people around you. Embrace

that mindset of gratitude and humility. Take a moment to reflect on the people who have contributed to your success thus far. Who has believed in you and supported you along the way? Who has provided guidance, encouragement, or even constructive criticism that helped you grow? Think about the mentors, teachers, colleagues, friends, and family members who have played a role in shaping your journey.

Now, imagine a world where acknowledgments and credit are not given. Picture a scenario where people take their accomplishments solely for themselves, disregarding the impact of others. How would that affect the relationships we have? How would it impact our motivation and willingness to help others? By recognizing and giving credit to those who have helped us succeed, we not only strengthen our relationships but also inspire a culture of reciprocity and support.

Acknowledging others is not just about saying a few words of gratitude. It goes beyond mere recognition; it involves truly understanding and appreciating the value of their contributions. It requires us to be attentive and observant, to acknowledge the small and big ways in which others have impacted our journey. By doing so, we create a positive ripple effect that encourages others to continue supporting and empowering us.

Moreover, the act of acknowledging and giving credit to others enhances our own self-awareness. It reminds us of our own fallibility and the interdependent nature of our lives. We come to realize that our success is not solely about our individual talents or efforts, but also about the opportunities, guidance, and support we receive from others. This realization cultivates humility and keeps us grounded, allowing us to continually learn and grow.

In addition to the personal benefits, acknowledging and giving credit to others also has profound professional advantages. In the workplace, recognizing the contributions of colleagues fosters a culture of collaboration and teamwork. It creates an environment where everyone feels valued and motivated to contribute their best. By highlighting the achievements of others, we inspire a sense of camaraderie, trust, and loyalty, which ultimately leads to increased productivity and innovation.

Furthermore, by acknowledging the contributions of others, we open doors to new opportunities and collaborations. The people we credit for their support and guidance become our advocates, spreading positive word-of-mouth and recommending us for future endeavors. They become part of our professional network, offering insights, connections, and potential partnerships that can further propel our success.

In our modern society, we often hear the phrase "self-made success." However, the truth is that it is impossible to achieve success alone. Whether it is the person who delivers your mail or the barista who makes your coffee every morning, there are countless individuals who contribute to our daily lives and play a part in our success.

It is easy to overlook these small gestures of kindness and support, but acknowledging them is crucial to our success. Acknowledging others is not only a reflection of our gratitude but also a sign of our emotional intelligence and awareness of the people around us. It helps us build stronger relationships with those around us, which is essential for success.

The art of giving credit and acknowledging others is not only limited to our personal relationships but also extends to our professional lives. Acknowledging colleagues, mentors, and industry experts who have contributed to our success not only builds stronger relationships but also helps us establish ourselves as a trustworthy and respected member of our professional community.

Furthermore, acknowledging others also helps us maintain a positive attitude and outlook. In our busy lives, we often forget to take a moment and appreciate the people around us. Acknowledging their contributions helps us cultivate an attitude of gratitude and optimism, which is essential for success.

Moreover, giving credit to others helps us avoid the pitfalls of arrogance and self-centeredness. It is easy to become self-absorbed when we achieve success, but acknowledging the people who helped us along the way helps us stay humble and grounded.

So, how do we give credit and acknowledge those who contribute to our success? It starts with awareness and gratitude. Take a moment to reflect on the people who have played a part in your success, whether big or small. It could be your family, friends, colleagues, or even strangers. Once you identify these individuals, take the time to express your gratitude and acknowledge their contributions.

One way to acknowledge others is to give credit where credit is due. If a colleague helped you with a project or a mentor gave you valuable advice, make sure to give them credit and acknowledge their contributions. It not only shows your appreciation but also helps build stronger relationships.

Another way to acknowledge others is to express your gratitude. Whether it is a simple thank you note or a heartfelt conversation, expressing your gratitude helps the people around you feel valued and appreciated.

Giving credit and acknowledging others is a crucial aspect of achieving success in life. It is essential to understand that success is not achieved in isolation, but rather as a result of the contributions of many individuals and factors. Acknowledging these contributions and being grateful for them can have a profound impact on our personal and professional lives. In this essay, we will explore the reasons why giving credit and acknowledgement are important for success and how it can be achieved.

Firstly, acknowledging others and giving credit helps to build positive relationships. When we acknowledge the contributions of others, it shows that we value their efforts and are grateful for their support. This creates a sense of mutual respect and appreciation, which can lead to stronger bonds and connections. In turn, these connections can lead to new opportunities, collaborations, and referrals, all of which are crucial for success in today's interconnected world.

Moreover, acknowledging others can boost morale and motivation. Everyone likes to be recognized and appreciated for their efforts. When we give credit to others, we create a positive environment that encourages individuals to continue to contribute and perform at their best. This can lead to higher levels of productivity, improved work quality, and greater job satisfaction. It can also lead to a sense of pride and ownership in the work being done, which can lead to greater engagement and commitment.

In addition, giving credit and acknowledgement can also help to build trust and credibility. When we give credit to others, we demonstrate our honesty and integrity. It shows that we are not solely focused on our own success but are also mindful of the contributions of others. This can lead to greater respect and trust from others, which can be invaluable in professional settings. Trust and credibility are essential for building strong relationships and creating opportunities for success.

Furthermore, giving credit and acknowledgement can help to foster a culture of gratitude. When we take the time to appreciate the contributions of others, it creates a positive and uplifting environment. It encourages individuals to be more mindful of the efforts of those around them and to express gratitude for their support. This can lead to a more positive and harmonious workplace, where individuals feel valued and appreciated.

Finally, giving credit and acknowledgement is simply the right thing to do. It is easy to take credit for our own successes and overlook the contributions of others. However, this is not only unfair but also counterproductive. By acknowledging others, we show that we are grateful for their support and recognize that we could not have achieved success without them. This can create a sense of humility and gratitude that can be a powerful driver of future success.

In conclusion, giving credit and acknowledgement is essential for success in life. It helps to build positive relationships, boost morale and motivation, build trust and credibility, foster a culture of gratitude, and is simply the right thing to do. By acknowledging the contributions of others and expressing gratitude for their support, we can create a more positive and supportive environment that is conducive to personal and professional growth.

One famous company known for acknowledging and giving credits to its employees is the software company Adobe Systems.

In 2012, Adobe implemented a program called the "Kickbox Program" which was designed to encourage innovation and creativity among employees. The program gave employees a box containing tools and resources, along with a $1,000 prepaid credit card to use towards developing their own ideas.

One employee, Mark Randall, used the Kickbox Program to develop a new product called Adobe Voice, which became a huge success. Rather than taking all the credit himself, Randall acknowledged and thanked the other employees who had helped him along the way, including the Kickbox Program team, his manager, and various colleagues who had given him feedback and support.

This culture of acknowledging and giving credit to employees has been a key factor in Adobe's success. It has helped to foster a sense of community and collaboration among employees, leading to more innovative ideas and products. It has also helped to create a more positive and supportive work environment, leading to higher employee morale and retention rates.

In addition, Adobe also regularly recognizes and celebrates the achievements of its employees through various programs and initiatives, including an annual "Adobe Founders' Award" which is given to employees who have made outstanding contributions to the company. By valuing and acknowledging the contributions of its employees, Adobe has built a strong culture of teamwork, innovation, and success.

One example of a company that is known for acknowledging and giving credit to employees for their success is Google.

Google has a company culture that values collaboration and teamwork, and this is reflected in their approach to giving credit. Employees are encouraged to share credit with others who have contributed to their success, and managers are expected to recognize and acknowledge the contributions of their team members.

One way that Google acknowledges and gives credit to employees is through their "Peer Bonus" program. This program allows employees to nominate their colleagues for a bonus based on their exceptional work or contributions to the team. This not only provides financial recognition for the employee, but also highlights their contributions to the wider team.

Google also has a culture of open communication and transparency, which allows employees to receive regular feedback and recognition for their work. This includes regular performance reviews and opportunities for employees to share their successes and accomplishments with their colleagues.

Overall, Google's approach to acknowledging and giving credit to employees has been a key factor in their success as a company. By valuing collaboration and recognizing the contributions of their team members, Google has built a culture of innovation and teamwork that has led to some of the most successful products and services in the tech industry.

Albert Einstein is one of the most renowned scientists in history. While he is known for his genius and groundbreaking contributions to the field of physics, he also recognized the importance of acknowledging and giving credit to the people around him who helped him achieve success.

Throughout his life and career, Einstein worked closely with a number of collaborators and colleagues who helped him in his research and experimentation. He often spoke highly of these individuals and credited them for their contributions to his work. For example, he worked closely with mathematician Marcel Grossmann on developing the theory of general relativity, and credited him for his key role in the project.

Einstein also acknowledged the support of his family, particularly his first wife, Mileva Maric, who was also a physicist and collaborator. In a letter to her, he wrote, "Without you, I am nothing. But with you, I am something. Together, we are everything."

Even after achieving great success and becoming a household name, Einstein remained humble and grateful to the people around him. In his acceptance speech for the Nobel Prize in Physics in 1922, he acknowledged the work of his colleagues and collaborators, saying, "Without them, I would have been like a deaf and dumb person."

Einstein's recognition of the contributions of those around him serves as an important lesson for all of us. No one achieves success alone, and it is important to acknowledge and give credit to the people who have helped us along the way. By doing so, we can show gratitude, build stronger relationships, and create a culture of collaboration and support.

ᑭᑭᑭ

Brian and Harvey were facing a major problem at their software development company - employees were leaving the company feeling unappreciated and undervalued. One day, an employee named Jack handed in his resignation letter citing lack of recognition for his hard work. Brian and Harvey were taken aback as Jack was one of their best programmers and losing him would be a huge blow to the company.

Determined to find a solution, Brian and Harvey had a brainstorming session and realized that they had been taking their employees for granted. They immediately put together a new policy for acknowledging hard work and giving credit where it was due. They implemented a program where they recognized the hard work of their employees and gave them credit where it was due.

Soon, the company saw a huge shift in the morale of the employees, who felt more appreciated and valued. Jack even reconsidered his resignation and decided to stay on with the company.

But Brian and Harvey didn't stop there - they realized that they were guilty of not giving credit to their own family members for their hard work and support. They made it a point to thank their spouses, children and parents for their support and the hard work they put in every day. This led to a happier and more fulfilling personal life for Brian and Harvey as well.

The new policy of giving credit and recognition to employees and loved ones helped the company grow and improve, and also strengthened the relationships of those involved.

ppp

By giving credit and acknowledging the efforts of others, we not only show our gratitude but also build stronger relationships and create a positive and supportive work environment. It also helps us to establish ourselves as a team player and leader, who values and appreciates the contributions of others.

1. Identify the people who have contributed to your success or helped you in achieving your goals.
2. Be specific about their contribution and the impact it had on your work or success.
3. Be genuine in your appreciation and give credit where it is due. Do not hesitate to acknowledge the efforts of others.
4. Choose an appropriate way to show your gratitude, such as a thank you note, an email, or a public acknowledgment.
5. Avoid taking credit for others' work or downplaying their contributions.
6. Make it a habit to regularly express gratitude and give credit to people who have supported you or contributed to your success

In conclusion, success is not an individual pursuit, but rather a collective effort. Acknowledging and giving credit to the people who have contributed to our achievements is a fundamental aspect of personal and professional growth. It cultivates gratitude, strengthens relationships, and fosters a culture of collaboration and support. So, as you continue your journey towards success, remember to pause and acknowledge those who have helped you along the way. Celebrate their contributions and express your gratitude. By doing so, you not only honor their impact but also pave the way for even greater accomplishments in the future.

 PPP

Chapter Summary:

In this chapter, we explored the importance of acknowledging and giving credit to others for their contributions to our success. It goes beyond mere recognition; it involves truly understanding and appreciating the value of their efforts. Acknowledging others not only creates a positive ripple effect but also enhances our self-awareness and cultivates humility. It builds trust, fosters collaboration, and boosts morale in professional settings. Additionally, giving credit to others opens doors to new opportunities and collaborations, as they become advocates and part of our professional network. We discussed the various ways to acknowledge others, such as giving credit where it's due, expressing gratitude, and fostering a culture of gratitude. Overall, acknowledging and giving credit to others is crucial for success, both personally and professionally, as it creates a supportive and positive environment that contributes to our growth and well-being.

Activity:

1. *Reflect on your journey: Take some time to reflect on your personal and professional journey and identify the individuals who have played a significant role in your success. Consider family, friends, colleagues, mentors, and even strangers who have impacted your life in meaningful ways.*

2. *Make a list: Create a list of the people you want to acknowledge and give credit to. Write down their names and the specific contributions they have made or the support they have provided.*

3. *Choose your approach: Decide how you would like to express your gratitude and give credit to each person on your list. There are various ways you can do this, such as: Write a heartfelt thank-you note or letter: Take the time to write a personalized message expressing your gratitude and acknowledging their specific contributions. Be specific and sincere in your words.Have a face-to-face conversation: If possible, schedule a meeting or call with the person to have a meaningful conversation. Express your appreciation verbally and let them know how their support has made a difference in your life.Publicly acknowledge their contributions: If appropriate, publicly recognize and give credit to the person in a team meeting, company newsletter, or social media platform. Share their achievements and how they have positively impacted your journey.*

4. *Follow through: Take action and reach out to each person on your list according to your chosen approach. Be genuine and heartfelt in your expressions of gratitude and credit.*

5. *Reflect on the experience: After completing each acknowledgment, take some time to reflect on how it felt to express your gratitude and give credit to others. Notice the impact it has on your own mindset and the relationships you have with the people you acknowledged.*

6. *Maintain a mindset of gratitude: Incorporate gratitude and acknowledgment into your daily life. Look for opportunities to recognize and appreciate the contributions of others regularly. This could be as simple as saying thank you, praising someone's efforts, or sharing credit in team settings.*

Remember, acknowledging and giving credit to others is an ongoing practice. By cultivating a mindset of gratitude and actively recognizing the contributions of others, you not only create a positive and supportive environment but also strengthen your own relationships and personal growth.

FIFTEEN

HEALTHY MIND, HEALTHY BODY: THE KEY TO LONGEVITY

"To keep the body in good health is a duty... otherwise, we shall not be able to keep our mind strong and clear." - Buddha

Imagine waking up on a beautiful sunny day, eager to start your day, but you realize that you have a sharp pain in your lower back. You try to ignore it, but it continues to nag at you throughout the day, affecting your productivity and mood. Despite the beautiful weather and your enthusiasm, you are unable to fully enjoy the day.

Now, consider waking up feeling physically fit and healthy, but your mind is tired and groggy. You struggle to focus on your work, and your thoughts wander aimlessly.

Even though your body is capable of handling any physical task, your mental fatigue prevents you from being fully engaged in your work and enjoying your day.

The examples above illustrate the importance of having both a healthy mind and body. It is essential to take care of both physical and mental health to lead a fulfilling life. A healthy mind and body work together to create a sense of balance and well-being, allowing individuals to achieve their full potential.

Physical fitness and mental health are interconnected. A healthy body can promote a healthy mind, and a healthy mind can promote a healthy body. Exercise and physical activity can improve mood, reduce stress and anxiety, and boost self-esteem, leading to a healthier mindset. Similarly, mental health can positively impact physical health. Positive thinking, healthy coping mechanisms, and stress management techniques can lead to better sleep patterns, reduced risk of chronic diseases, and increased longevity.

The benefits of a healthy mind and body go beyond personal well-being. A healthy mind and body also improve work productivity, social relationships, and overall quality of life. When individuals are physically and mentally fit, they have the energy, focus, and motivation to accomplish tasks and pursue their goals. They are also more likely to build positive relationships and enjoy social interactions, contributing to a fulfilling life.

The Veda and Purana, ancient Indian texts, have long emphasized the importance of a healthy mind and body for achieving success and fulfilment in life. These texts offer a holistic approach to achieving optimal health, which encompasses physical, mental, and spiritual well-being. In Vedic science, the body is viewed as a temple, and it is essential to maintain it in good health to achieve one's life goals. The ancient Indian system of Ayurveda is based on the concept of balance and harmony, and it emphasizes the importance of a healthy diet, physical exercise, and mental practices such as meditation and yoga to achieve overall well-being.

The practice of yoga, which originated in ancient India, is a well-known system of physical, mental, and spiritual practices that promote good health and well-being. Yoga involves physical postures, breathing exercises, and meditation techniques that are designed to improve strength, flexibility, and mental clarity. Through regular practice, individuals can achieve a balance between mind and body, which is essential for achieving success in various aspects of life.

In addition to physical practices, Vedic science also emphasizes the importance of mental and spiritual practices for achieving a healthy mind and body. The practice of meditation, for example, is believed to reduce stress and anxiety, improve focus and concentration, and promote emotional stability. The Veda and Purana also emphasize the importance of positive thinking and the power of the mind to influence one's life experiences.

Overall, the Veda and Purana offer a comprehensive approach to achieving a healthy mind and body for success. By incorporating physical, mental, and spiritual practices into daily life, individuals can achieve a state of optimal health and well-being, which is essential for achieving success and fulfilment in life.

In ancient Greece, the concept of "eudaimonia" was central to the idea of holistic health and was believed to be essential for achieving success and fulfilment in life. Eudaimonia, which translates to "happiness" or "flourishing," was achieved through a balance between physical, mental, and spiritual well-being.

The Greeks believed that a healthy mind and body were essential for achieving eudaimonia. Physical health was achieved through regular exercise, a balanced diet, and the avoidance of harmful substances. Mental health was achieved through practices such as philosophy, meditation, and self-reflection, which helped individuals to develop self-awareness, emotional stability, and resilience in the face of adversity.

The Greeks also believed in the importance of spiritual well-being for achieving eudaimonia. This was achieved through the practice of religion and the cultivation of virtues such as wisdom, courage, and compassion. The Greeks believed that cultivating these virtues would lead to a life of meaning and purpose, which was essential for achieving eudaimonia.

The concept of eudaimonia was central to the teachings of Greek philosophers such as Aristotle, who believed that achieving eudaimonia was the ultimate goal of human life. According to Aristotle, eudaimonia was achieved through the cultivation of virtues and the pursuit of intellectual and moral excellence. He believed that by living a life of virtue and pursuing excellence in all aspects of life, individuals could achieve eudaimonia and experience true happiness and fulfilment.

The concept of a healthy body and mind is present in many world ancient scriptures and has been emphasized by different cultures throughout history, for example in Chinese culture, the concept of "Qi" or "Chi" is central to the idea of optimal health. Traditional Chinese medicine emphasizes the importance of balancing Qi through various practices such as acupuncture, herbal medicine, and tai chi to achieve overall well-being.

According to Traditional Chinese Medicine (TCM), imbalances or blockages in the flow of Qi can result in various health problems. Therefore, the goal of TCM is to balance and restore the flow of Qi in the body through practices such as acupuncture, herbal medicine, and tai chi.

Acupuncture involves the insertion of thin needles into specific points on the body to stimulate the flow of Qi and restore balance. Herbal medicine uses natural remedies made from plants, minerals, and animal products to support the body's natural healing processes and restore balance. Tai chi is a form of martial arts that involves slow, gentle movements and deep breathing exercises designed to promote the flow of Qi and enhance physical and mental well-being.

In Japanese culture, a similar concept to Qi is known as "ki" or "chi," which is also considered a vital force that flows through the body and is essential for maintaining optimal health and well-being. Traditional Japanese medicine emphasizes the importance of balancing ki through practices such as acupuncture, herbal medicine, and shiatsu massage.

In Islamic scripture, the Quran emphasizes the importance of maintaining good health and taking care of the body as a form of worship. It encourages the consumption of wholesome and natural foods, regular exercise, and proper rest to maintain optimal health.

Overall, the concept of a healthy body and mind is a common theme in many world ancient scriptures and cultures. Whether it is called eudaimonia, Qi, ki, prana, or another name, the goal is the same: to balance and restore the flow of vital energy to achieve overall well-being.

The connection between a healthy mind and a healthy body is well-established, and it is no surprise that this connection extends to achieving success in life. A healthy mind, one that is positive, resilient, and focused, can help individuals overcome obstacles, manage stress, and stay motivated towards achieving their goals. On the other hand, a healthy body, fueled by proper nutrition and exercise, can provide the physical stamina and energy needed to pursue success.

Research has shown that a positive mental attitude has significant health benefits, such as reducing stress, boosting the immune system, and increasing lifespan. One study conducted by the Harvard School of Public Health found that individuals with a positive outlook on life had a 50% lower risk of heart disease than those with a negative outlook. Another study conducted by researchers at the University of Pittsburgh found that optimism was associated with lower levels of inflammation, a key factor in the development of chronic diseases.

Chronic stress, on the other hand, has been linked to a host of negative health outcomes, including an increased risk of heart disease, depression, and anxiety. Stressful situations can trigger the release of cortisol, a hormone that can lead to inflammation and damage to the body's cells. This can lead to a cycle of negative thinking, which can further exacerbate stress and lead to more negative health outcomes.

The food we eat also has a direct impact on our physical and mental health. A healthy diet, rich in fruits, vegetables, lean protein, and whole grains, provides the essential nutrients needed to support the body's functions and maintain overall health. In addition, research has shown that certain nutrients, such as omega-3 fatty acids and B vitamins, can have a positive effect on mental health.

For example, a study conducted by researchers at the University of Pittsburgh found that omega-3 fatty acids, found in fatty fish, can help reduce symptoms of depression and anxiety. Another study conducted by the University of Sydney found that a diet rich in B vitamins, such as those found in leafy greens and whole grains, can help improve cognitive function and reduce the risk of dementia.

Regular physical activity has numerous health benefits, including improving cardiovascular health, reducing the risk of chronic diseases, and boosting mental health. Exercise releases endorphins, the body's natural feel-good chemicals, which can help reduce stress, anxiety, and depression. Studies have also shown that regular exercise can help improve cognitive function, including memory and attention.

A sedentary lifestyle, on the other hand, can have negative effects on both physical and mental health. Sitting for long periods of time has been linked to an increased risk of obesity, heart disease, and other chronic illnesses. In addition, a lack of physical activity can lead to decreased cognitive function and an increased risk of depression and anxiety.

To achieve a healthy mind and body, it is important to develop healthy habits such as regular exercise, a balanced diet, and stress management techniques. This can include activities such as yoga, meditation, or mindfulness practices, as well as seeking professional help if needed. Setting realistic goals, practicing gratitude, and maintaining social connections can also help foster a positive mental attitude and improve overall well-being.

In conclusion, the link between a healthy mind and body is essential for success in all aspects of life. By prioritizing our mental and physical health, we can cultivate the resilience, motivation, and energy needed to achieve our goals and lead fulfilling lives.

The mind-body connection refers to the relationship between the mental and physical aspects of our being. It is a two-way street, meaning that the state of our mind affects the state of our body, and vice versa. The connection between the mind and body is so strong that a positive mental attitude has been shown to have significant health benefits, such as reducing stress, boosting the immune system, and even increasing lifespan.

The food we eat has a direct impact on our physical and mental health. A healthy diet, rich in fruits, vegetables, lean protein, and whole grains, provides the essential nutrients needed to support the body's functions and maintain overall health. In addition, research has shown that certain nutrients, such as omega-3 fatty acids and B vitamins, can have a positive effect on mental health.

For example, a study conducted by researchers at the University of Pittsburgh found that omega-3 fatty acids, found in fatty fish, can help reduce symptoms of depression and anxiety. Another study conducted by the University of Sydney found that a diet rich in B vitamins, such as those found in leafy greens and whole grains, can help improve cognitive function and reduce the risk of dementia.

On the other hand, a diet high in processed foods, saturated fats, and sugar can have negative effects on both physical and mental health. Research has linked a diet high in processed foods to an increased risk of obesity, heart disease, and other chronic illnesses. In addition, a diet high in sugar has been linked to an increased risk of depression and anxiety.

Regular physical activity has numerous health benefits, including improving cardiovascular health, reducing the risk of chronic diseases, and boosting mental health. Exercise releases endorphins, the body's natural feel-good chemicals, which can help reduce stress, anxiety, and depression.

Studies have also shown that regular exercise can help improve cognitive function, including memory and attention. A study conducted by researchers at the University of British Columbia found that regular aerobic exercise can help increase the size of the hippocampus, a region of the brain responsible for memory.

On the other hand, a sedentary lifestyle can have negative effects on both physical and mental health. Sitting for long periods of time has been linked to an increased risk of obesity, heart disease, and other chronic illnesses. In addition, a lack of physical activity can lead to decreased cognitive function and increased risk of depression and anxiety.

Achieving a healthy mind and body can seem like a daunting task, but with the right strategies and mindset, it is entirely possible. Here are some strategies for achieving a healthy mind and body:

1. Make exercise a priority: Regular physical activity is essential for maintaining a healthy body and mind. Aim for at least 30 minutes of moderate exercise per day, such as brisk walking, cycling, or swimming. Incorporate strength training exercises two to three times per week to build muscle and improve bone density.

2. Eat a balanced diet: Proper nutrition is essential for fueling the body and maintaining good health. Eat a variety of fruits, vegetables, whole grains, lean protein, and healthy fats to ensure that your body is getting all

the essential nutrients it needs.

3. Manage stress: Chronic stress can have negative effects on both physical and mental health. Learn to manage stress through techniques such as meditation, yoga, deep breathing exercises, or seeking the help of a mental health professional.

4. Get enough sleep: Adequate sleep is essential for overall health and well-being. Aim for seven to eight hours of sleep per night, and establish a consistent sleep routine to help regulate your body's natural sleep-wake cycle.

5. Practice mindfulness: Mindfulness practices such as meditation, yoga, or mindfulness-based stress reduction can help improve mental health and reduce stress levels. These practices can also help cultivate a sense of inner peace and well-being.

6. Cultivate social connections: Social connections are essential for mental and emotional well-being. Make an effort to connect with friends and loved ones regularly, join a social group or club, or volunteer in your community.

7. Set realistic goals: Setting goals that are challenging but achievable can help cultivate motivation and a sense of purpose. Whether it's a fitness goal, career goal, or personal goal, create a plan of action and work towards achieving it one step at a time.

8. Practice gratitude: Gratitude practices such as journaling, expressing gratitude to others, or practicing mindfulness of gratitude can help cultivate a positive mindset and improve overall well-being.

In summary, achieving a healthy mind and body requires a holistic approach that encompasses regular exercise, proper nutrition, stress management, good sleep hygiene, mindfulness practices, social connections, realistic goal-setting, and gratitude practices. By incorporating these strategies into your daily routine, you can cultivate a sense of well-being and achieve success in all aspects of your life.

In Hinduism, the concept of the body and mind as a means of spiritual elevation is a central tenet of the faith. According to Hindu philosophy, the ultimate goal of human life is to achieve moksha(salvation), or liberation from the cycle of birth and death. This can only be attained by elevating the soul to a higher state of consciousness, which requires a dedicated and disciplined practice of sadhana(methodical discipline to attain desired knowledge or goal), or spiritual discipline.

The body, in Hinduism, is seen as a tool for spiritual practice and sadhana. The physical body is seen as a temporary vessel for the soul, which is eternal and divine. The body is therefore not the ultimate reality, but rather a means to an end - the end being the attainment of moksha.

The practice of sadhana involves using the body and mind to achieve a state of spiritual purity and clarity. This involves practices such as yoga, meditation, fasting, and self-discipline. By mastering the body and mind, one can elevate the soul and achieve a higher state of consciousness.

In Hinduism, the concept of karma also plays a key role in the idea of spiritual elevation. Karma refers to the concept of cause and effect - the idea that our actions have consequences, both in this life and in future lives. By performing good deeds and leading a virtuous life, one can accumulate positive karma and move closer to moksha.

Overall, the concept of the body and mind as a means of spiritual elevation in Hinduism is a profound and deeply ingrained idea. By using the body and mind as tools for spiritual practice, one can achieve a higher state of consciousness and ultimately attain moksha - the ultimate goal of human life.

ppp

Brian and Harvey, the dynamic duo behind a leading software company, had spent decades building and scaling their business to the top. However, in the process of achieving their goals, they completely neglected their own health. They had become so focused on the success of their company that they had forgotten to take care of themselves.

Their hectic work schedule had left them with no time for exercise or healthy eating habits. They would often skip meals or resort to fast food, and had no regular physical activity in their routine. This neglect had also taken a toll on their mental health, leaving them stressed and exhausted.

One day, while working on a new project, one of their employees suddenly collapsed due to stress and exhaustion. This incident served as a wake-up call for Brian and Harvey, and they realized that they had been neglecting their own health as well.

Feeling guilty and concerned, they decided to create awareness about the importance of mental and physical health among their employees. They organized a company-wide health campaign, encouraging everyone to take breaks, eat healthy, exercise, and practice mindfulness.

To make things fun, they even started a weekly "fitness challenge" where employees competed to see who could walk the most steps or do the most push-ups. They also started a "healthy snack" initiative, where they provided free fresh fruits and veggies for employees to snack on instead of junk food.

With the help of these initiatives, Brian and Harvey saw a remarkable improvement in the overall well-being of their employees, including themselves. They realized that taking care of one's mental and physical health is just as important as working hard, and it's important to prioritize self-care in order to be successful in the long run.

ᐯᐯᐯ

The concept of using the body and mind as tools for spiritual elevation in Hinduism is not limited to achieving moksha, but can also be applied to achieving success in one's personal and professional life.

By incorporating the principles of sadhana into our daily routine, we can cultivate discipline, focus, and resilience, which are essential qualities for achieving success. Practices such as yoga and meditation can help us manage stress and anxiety, improve our focus and concentration, and boost our energy levels, allowing us to tackle challenges with clarity and ease.

In addition, the concept of karma can be applied to our daily lives by practicing selflessness and kindness towards others. By performing good deeds and leading a virtuous life, we can accumulate positive karma, which can attract positive energy and opportunities into our lives.

Another important aspect of the Hindu philosophy of spiritual elevation is the idea of detachment from the outcome of our actions. This means that we should focus on performing our actions to the best of our ability, without becoming attached to the results or outcomes. This can help us maintain a sense of inner peace and equanimity, even in the face of challenges and setbacks.

Furthermore, the idea of using the body and mind as tools for spiritual elevation can also help us develop a sense of purpose and meaning in our lives. By aligning our actions with our values and goals, we can create a sense of direction and focus that can help us achieve success and fulfilment.

ᗏᗏᗏ

Chapter Summary:

In this chapter, we explored the importance of maintaining a healthy mind and body. We delved into various ancient scriptures and cultural beliefs that emphasized the interconnectedness of physical and mental health. The Veda and Purana provided insights from ancient India, highlighting the holistic approach of Ayurveda and the transformative power of yoga. We also examined the Greek concept of eudaimonia, which underscored the significance of balancing physical, mental, and spiritual well-being. Additionally, we explored the Chinese and Japanese perspectives, which emphasized the importance of harmonizing Qi and ki through practices like acupuncture, herbal medicine, and tai chi. Islamic scripture also emphasized the value of good health and self-care.

Throughout this chapter, we discovered that scientific research supports the positive impact of a healthy mind and body. Studies revealed that maintaining a positive mental attitude contributes to reduced stress, strengthened immune systems, and increased longevity. Chronic stress, on the other hand, was found to have detrimental effects on health. Furthermore, we learned that a balanced diet, rich in essential nutrients, and regular exercise are crucial for physical and mental well-being. Exercise releases endorphins, fostering mental well-being, while sedentary lifestyles were associated with negative outcomes.

To achieve a healthy mind and body, it is essential to adopt healthy habits such as regular exercise, a balanced diet, and stress management techniques. Engaging in activities like yoga, meditation, and mindfulness practices can be beneficial, as well as seeking professional help when needed. Setting realistic goals, practicing gratitude, and nurturing social connections were also identified as effective strategies for fostering a positive mental attitude and improving overall well-being.

By integrating the wisdom from ancient scriptures, cultural beliefs, and scientific research, we can understand the profound significance of a healthy mind and body. Taking care of both aspects allows us to lead fulfilling lives, pursue our goals, and enjoy meaningful relationships. As we conclude this chapter, let us carry forward the knowledge and insights gained to prioritize our mental and physical well-being, aiming for a balanced and harmonious life.

Activity:

1. *Engage in Regular Physical Activity: Incorporate at least 30 minutes of moderate-intensity exercise into your daily routine. This can include activities like brisk walking, jogging, cycling, swimming, or engaging in a sport you enjoy. Regular physical activity promotes cardiovascular health, reduces the risk of chronic diseases, and improves mental well-being.*

2. *Practice Mindfulness and Meditation: Set aside a few minutes each day to engage in mindfulness or meditation practices. Find a quiet and comfortable space, focus on your breath, and allow your mind to calm and center. This practice can reduce stress, increase self-awareness, and enhance mental clarity.*

3. *Maintain a Balanced Diet: Consume a diet rich in fruits, vegetables, whole grains, lean proteins, and healthy fats. Avoid processed foods and excessive sugar and salt. Ensure you stay hydrated by drinking an adequate amount of water throughout the day. A balanced diet provides essential nutrients for physical and mental well-being.*

4. *Prioritize Quality Sleep: Establish a consistent sleep schedule and aim for 7-8 hours of quality sleep each night. Create a relaxing bedtime routine that includes activities like reading a book, taking a warm bath, or practicing relaxation techniques. Sufficient sleep promotes cognitive function, emotional well-being, and physical health.*

5. *Cultivate Positive Thinking: Practice positive affirmations and gratitude exercises daily. Focus on the good in your life and express appreciation for the things you have. Replace negative self-talk with positive and empowering statements. Cultivating positive thinking can improve your mental attitude, reduce stress, and enhance overall well-being.*

6. *Seek Social Connections: Nurture meaningful relationships with family, friends, and community. Engage in social activities, join clubs or organizations, or participate in group classes or events that align with your interests. Connecting with others fosters a sense of belonging, reduces feelings of loneliness, and promotes overall happiness.*

7. *Limit Screen Time and Digital Detox: Reduce the amount of time spent on electronic devices, such as smartphones, computers, and television. Take breaks from screens and engage in activities that promote relaxation and creativity, such as reading a book, going for a walk-in nature, or pursuing a hobby.*

8. *Practice Stress Management Techniques: Explore various stress management techniques such as deep breathing exercises, progressive muscle relaxation, journaling, or*

engaging in hobbies or activities that bring you joy and relaxation. Find what works best for you to alleviate stress and incorporate these practices into your daily routine.

9. *Engage in Lifelong Learning: Stimulate your mind by engaging in activities that promote learning and personal growth. Read books, listen to podcasts, take up a new hobby, or enroll in courses or workshops. Lifelong learning enhances cognitive function, keeps the mind active, and fosters a sense of fulfilment.*

10. *Seek Professional Help if Needed: If you are facing challenges with your mental or physical health, do not hesitate to seek professional help. Consult with a healthcare provider, therapist, or counsellor who can provide guidance, support, and personalized recommendations to address your specific needs.*

Remember, achieving a healthy mind and body is a journey, and it's important to be patient and kind to yourself along the way. By incorporating these activities into your daily life, you can gradually create a lifestyle that promotes optimal well-being and helps you reach your full potential.

ppp

Book Summary

ﬡﬡﬡ

"Success is not final, failure is not fatal: It is the courage to continue that counts." - Winston Churchill

ﬡﬡﬡ

The book has an example of two characters named Brian and Harvey, who could also represent the Brain and Heart, respectively. As humans, we make decisions based on our analytical thinking, critical reasoning, knowledge, and other influencing factors. However, sometimes we make decisions based on intuition, where we feel in our heart that something is right. Brian and Harvey are similar in this regard.

Brian and Harvey's journey from their early days until they achieved success involved the application of the 15 principles mentioned in the book. Let's take a closer look at how they applied each principle and how we can apply them in our own lives.

1. Mastering Time Management - Brian and Harvey understood the importance of time management and developed effective techniques to prioritize their tasks. We can learn from them by setting clear goals and creating a schedule that allows us to maximize our time and productivity.
2. Empowering Growth - Both Brian and Harvey were

committed to lifelong learning and continuously sought to expand their knowledge. We can follow their example by investing time in reading, attending seminars, and developing new skills.

3. Building Strong Networks - Harvey was a master at building genuine relationships and networking, while Brian focused on building a strong professional network. We can learn from them by building connections with like-minded individuals and leveraging those relationships to achieve our goals.

4. Sailing the Internet Seas - Brian and Harvey were both tech-savvy and utilized the internet to their advantage. We can follow their example by using technology to streamline our work, stay informed, and connect with others.

5. No Comparison - Both Brian and Harvey understood the dangers of constantly comparing themselves to others and instead focused on their own growth and progress. We can apply this principle by recognizing our own unique strengths and focusing on self-improvement.

6. Staying Humble - Despite their success, Brian and Harvey remained humble and grounded, treating others with respect and kindness. We can learn from them by cultivating humility and recognizing the value in every person we encounter.

7. Honesty and Truth - Honesty was a core value for both Brian and Harvey, and they believed in living with integrity and transparency. We can follow their example by always telling the truth and being honest in our interactions with others.

8. Punctuality and Ethics - Brian and Harvey recognized the importance of being reliable and ethical in all their dealings, including showing up on time for

appointments and meetings. We can apply this principle by honoring our commitments and being accountable for our actions.

9. Grabbing Opportunities - Both Brian and Harvey were quick to seize opportunities and take calculated risks in pursuit of their goals. We can follow their example by being open to new opportunities and taking action when we see potential for growth.

10. Staying Persistance- Despite facing setbacks and obstacles, Brian and Harvey persisted in their pursuit of success. We can apply this principle by maintaining a positive attitude and persevering in the face of challenges.

11. Balancing Work and Life - Brian and Harvey understood the importance of achieving a healthy work-life balance, and prioritized their personal lives alongside their professional goals. We can learn from them by taking breaks when we need them, prioritizing self-care, and cultivating fulfilling relationships.

12. Prioritizing Self-Realization - Both Brian and Harvey were committed to personal growth and self-realization, recognizing the importance of developing their own unique identities. We can follow their example by pursuing our passions and developing a sense of purpose in our lives.

13. Building Personal Brand - Brian and Harvey both understood the importance of building a strong personal brand, and consistently presented themselves in a positive and professional manner. We can apply this principle by cultivating our own unique brand and showcasing our strengths and accomplishments.

14. Giving Credit - Both Brian and Harvey recognized the contributions of others and gave credit where it was due.

We can follow their example by acknowledging the efforts of others and showing gratitude for their contributions.

15. Emphasizing Healthy Mind and Body - Finally, Brian and Harvey understood the importance of a healthy mind and body, and made efforts to maintain their physical and mental health. We can apply this principle by prioritizing exercise, good nutrition, and self-care in our lives.

ᏢᏢᏢ

Author's Words

"Infuse your work with passion and dedication, treating it as a sacred calling that resonates with the depths of your being. But hold in your heart the wisdom that work is but a single brushstroke on the canvas of your expansive life's masterpiece." - Vikram Varakhedi

ᐩᐩᐩ

Thank you for taking the time to read "Metanoia" and exploring the 15 principles for success discussed within its pages. It is my sincere hope that the insights shared in this book have resonated with you and provided meaningful guidance for your personal and professional journey.

As you reflect on these principles, I invite you to contemplate how you can integrate them into your own life in practical and impactful ways. True transformation and growth come from applying knowledge and wisdom to our daily actions. By embracing these principles, you have the power to unlock your full potential and embark on a path towards greater success and fulfilment.

I encourage you to extend this gift of knowledge to others who may benefit from it. Share this book with your friends, colleagues, and acquaintances, and empower them to pursue their own goals and dreams. By spreading these insights, you become a catalyst for positive change in the lives of those around you.

Always remember that success encompasses much more than mere external achievements or material possessions. It is about living a life driven by purpose, meaning, and a deep sense of fulfilment. By cultivating the right mindset and embracing these principles, you have the ability to shape the life you genuinely desire and deserve.

Thank you for joining me on this remarkable journey towards success. I extend my heartfelt wishes for your future endeavours, and I eagerly anticipate witnessing the extraordinary accomplishments you will achieve.

ಭಾರತೀರಮಣ ಮುಖ್ಯಪ್ರಾಣಾಂತರ್ಗತ
ಶ್ರೀಕೃಷ್ಣಾರ್ಪಣಮಸ್ತು

Vikram Varakhedi

ೡೡೡ

Appendix: Additional Resources

ᐅᐅᐅ

• 1.

Mastering Time Management

Eat That Frog!: 21 Great Ways to Stop Procrastinating and Get More Done in Less Time by Brian Tracy

The 7 Habits of Highly Effective People: Powerful Lessons in Personal Change by Stephen R. Covey

2. *Gaining Knowledge*

The Power of Habit: Why We Do What We Do in Life and Business by Charles Duhigg

Mindset: The New Psychology of Success by Carol S. Dweck

3.

Building Strong Networks

Never Eat Alone: And Other Secrets to Success, One Relationship at a Time by Keith Ferrazzi

How to Win Friends and Influence People by Dale Carnegie

4.

Using the Internet Wisely

Deep Work: Rules for Focused Success in a Distracted World by Cal Newport

The Shallows: What the Internet Is Doing to Our Brains by Nicholas Carr

5.

Stopping Comparisons

The Art of Possibility: Transforming Professional and Personal Life by Rosamund Stone Zander and Benjamin Zander

The Gifts of Imperfection: Let Go of Who You Think You're Supposed to Be and Embrace Who You Are by Brené Brown

6.

Staying Humble

Humilitas: A Lost Key to Life, Love, and Leadership by John Dickson

The Little Book of Talent: 52 Tips for Improving Your Skills by Daniel Coyle

7.

Valuing Truth and Honesty

The Truth About Lies: The Illusion of Honesty and the Evolution of Deceit by Gerd Gigerenzer

The Honest Truth About Dishonesty: How We Lie to Everyone - Especially Ourselves by Dan Ariely

8.

Punctuality and Ethics

The Power of Ethical Management by Ken Blanchard and Norman Vincent Peale

Time Management: Increase Your Personal Productivity and Effectiveness by Harvard Business Review

9.

Grabbing Opportunities

The Lean Startup: How Today's Entrepreneurs Use Continuous Innovation to Create Radically Successful Businesses by Eric Ries

Drive: The Surprising Truth About What Motivates Us by Daniel H. Pink

10.

Staying Persistent

Grit: The Power of Passion and Perseverance by Angela Duckworth

Mind Gym: An Athlete's Guide to Inner Excellence by Gary Mack and David Casstevens

11.

Balancing Work and Life

The 4-Hour Work Week: Escape 9-5, Live Anywhere, and Join the New Rich by Timothy Ferriss
The Happiness Project: Or, Why I Spent a Year Trying to Sing in the Morning, Clean My Closets, Fight Right, Read Aristotle, and Generally Have More Fun by Gretchen Rubin

12.

Prioritizing Self-Realization

The Alchemist by Paulo Coelho
Man's Search for Meaning by Viktor E. Frankl

13.

Building Personal Brand

Building a StoryBrand: Clarify Your Message So Customers Will Listen by Donald Miller
The Brand Gap: How to Bridge the Distance Between Business Strategy and Design by Marty Neumeier

14.

Giving Credit

The Power of Giving: How Giving Back Enriches Us All by Azim Jamal and Harvey McKinnon
The Thank You Economy by Gary Vaynerchuk

15.

Emphasizing Healthy Mind and Body

Spark: The Revolutionary New Science of Exercise and the Brain by John J. Ratey and Eric Hagerman

The 7 Habits of Highly Effective People: Powerful Lessons

ϷϷϷ